BUSINESS MATTERS

the business course with a lexical approach

Mark Powell

LTP
BUSINESS

Language Teaching Publications

35 Church Road, Hove, BN3 2BE, England

Students' Book
ISBN 1 899396 10 1
© LTP 1996
Reprinted 1996

Cassette
ISBN 1 899396 20 9

Teachers' Resource Book
ISBN 1 899396 15 2

NO UNAUTHORISED PHOTOCOPYING

The Author

Mark Powell has taught English in the UK and throughout Europe. He has extensive experience teaching business English and is a well-known teacher-trainer in this field.

Acknowledgements

The author would like to thank Jimmie Hill for his good sense and editorial expertise; Michael Lewis for his insight and sound advice; Charlie La Fond and the teachers at Business Language Center, Vienna, for their positive feedback and encouragement; and Giselle for her support during the writing of this book.
Photographs courtesy of: British Airways and Adrian Meredith Photography, Robert Harding Picture Library, FPG International, Virgin Atlantic, Zefa Picture Library, The Environmental Picture Library, Photoworld, The Japan Information and Cultural Centre – London, Toby Adamson, David Hoffman, Paul Van Dyke and Southern Publishing – Brighton.
Design by Anna Macleod
Cover photograph by Richard Bryant, Arcaid
Typeset by Blackmore Typesetting Services, Brighton
Printed in England by Commercial Colour Press, London E7

TO THE STUDENT

A New Approach

Business Matters is based on the latest research into the language of business. At your level of English you do not need to spend a lot of time learning more grammar or vocabulary. What you need is the ability to combine words, many of which you already know, into the phrases and expressions which are the basis of business English. Business Matters is the fast-track to fluency in the special English of business.

Getting Started

Each unit of Business Matters explores a different international business issue. You can study them in any order. You may wish to work through the book from the beginning to the end or you may choose those units which are of most interest to you and work on those first. Study the contents list on the next four pages to discover the topics and the key language taught in each unit.

If you are working in class

Take every opportunity to discuss the issues raised in your course with your fellow students and teacher or trainer. By talking about what interests you or surprises you in the articles, you will be re-cycling a lot of the language you need to learn.

Most of the exercises on the Language Focus pages can be done in class or at home. Make sure you do at home the ones which you do not do in class.

At the end of each unit there is a fluency activity to give you the chance to use the language you have learned in the unit. Sometimes they need some preparation – just like a task at work. Make sure you understand what you need to do. It is a good idea to read the instructions at home first.

If you are working alone

How much time can you realistically spend studying at home? An hour twice a week is better than eight hours once a month. Resist the temptation to read all the articles first. Work on one at a time and do the exercises which follow it. This will keep your interest level up and help you to learn any new language in easy stages. Don't be afraid to do the exercises aloud to yourself or to summarize what you have read out loud.

Talking to yourself is a superb way of revising your English when you have nobody else to talk to!

The Articles

The articles at the beginning of each unit are the most important part of this course. They have been carefully written to include lots of useful language. Most of the exercises are based on them. By referring back to the articles you will find the language work easier, and you will be reading the language in context. Always refer back to the text – rather than look the answers up in the key.

The Cassette

All the articles have been recorded on cassette. Listening to a recording of an article a few days after reading it is an excellent way of reminding yourself of the most useful language. Read an article, then listen to it. Listen to it, then read it. Leave it for a few days and listen again. The more you listen and read, the better!

Before Unit One

Some of the exercises in this book may be different from those you have done in the past. Before you start the units we recommend that you study page 8 – Before Unit One. This introduces you to several key ideas in the English of business which will help you develop your fluency. In particular, you will learn how important word partnerships are.

CONTENTS

Page 8   Before Unit One

Page 9   Unit 1: Global Marketing

Text   *Going Global:*   how the world's biggest advertisers have responded to the
                increasing globalization of markets

Language Focus Keywords: *marketing, market, advertising, commercial*
                Sentence starters for *presentations*
                Adverbs of degree
                Word grammar: forming verbs with *-ise / -ize*

Discussion Topics The effectiveness of advertising, market leaders, business ethics, choice of
                   brand names

Fluency Work   *Case Studies:* BP, Pepsi, Rolls-Royce – what would you have done?

Page 17   Unit 2: Enterprise

Text   *Entrepreneurs:* the hero status of the entrepreneur and the secrets of
                entrepreneurial success

Language Focus Word partnerships in the context of entrepreneurial skills
                Business grammar: *reporting verbs, gerund / infinitive expressions, prepositional
                verbs*

Discussion Topics Enterprise within large organizations, managers vs entrepreneurs, personal
                   successes

Fluency Work   *Business Venture:* starting a new business, drawing up and presenting a
                business plan

Page 25   Unit 3: Monopolies

Text   *Diamonds are Forever:* the rights and wrongs of one of the world's most
                monopolistic industries

Language Focus Market expressions, trade terms
                Word grammar: verbs prefixed by *over-, under-, out-*
                Word partnerships in the context of *supply and demand*

Discussion Topics How companies are affected by economic recession and boom, trade wars, the
                   free market

Fluency Work   *The State of the Market:* current market trends
                Press Conference: De Beers face the press, follow-up letter

Page 33   Unit 4: Corporate Structure

Text   *Re-engineering the Corporation:* how companies are having to restructure
                dramatically to keep pace with the changing world of business

Language Focus Keyword: *company*
                Word partnerships with phrasal verbs
                Business grammar: *conditional expressions*
                Sentence starters for *forecasting*

Discussion Topics Management structure, autonomy in the workplace, mergers and acquisitions,
                   the promotion ladder

Fluency Work   *Troubleshooter:* presenting recommendations for corporate restructuring to the
                management of an ailing engineering company

CONTENTS

Page 41   **Unit 5: Brand Management**

Text   *Brand Wars:* in retail marketing the battle is on amongst the brand leaders, the own-label products and the pirates

Language Focus   Keywords: *market, brand, consumer*
Word partnerships in the context of *brand management*
Business idioms: expressions to do with *warfare* and *combat*

Discussion Topics   Household names, upmarket and downmarket goods, product proliferation, dealing with sales letters

Fluency Work   *Product Development:* conceptualizing and presenting a new product to compete with an established brand name

Page 49   **Unit 6: Prices and Commodities**

Text   *If the Price is Right… :* the factors that determine the price of goods and services are alarmingly unpredictable

Language Focus   Keywords: *price, trade, profit, compete*
Fixed expressions in the context of *price* and *money*
Link words
The language of *trends and developments*

Discussion Topics   Bargaining, profit margins, factors influencing pricing policy, taxes and subsidies

Fluency Work   *The Commodities Game:* with a million dollars to spend, teams buy and sell commodities in the hope of making their fortune

Page 57   **Unit 7: Corporate Entertaining**

Text   *Looking after the Twenty Percent:* is corporate entertainment just a form of bribery or is it a legitimate part of a company's overall marketing effort?

Language Focus   Word partnerships in the context of *corporate entertainment*
Describing food and drink
Fixed expressions with *deal*

Discussion Topics   Above-the-line and below-the-line marketing, corporate gift-giving, the business lunch

Fluency Work   *Mixing Business with Pleasure:* a supplier takes a client out to dinner in order to renegotiate a contract

Page 65   **Unit 8: Innovation**

Texts   *Bright Ideas / The Lateral Thinker:* what are the optimum conditions for creativity in business and can creativity be learnt?

Language Focus   Keywords: *research, problems, ideas*
Word partnerships with *make* and *do*
Quantifiers

Discussion Topics   New product development, problem-solving techniques, dealing with objections raised in meetings

Fluency Work   *Brainstorm:* can you come up with a commercial application for an apparently useless product?

CONTENTS

Page 73   **Unit 9: Sales Techniques**

Texts   *The Soft Sell / The Hard Sell:* selling is at the heart of successful business, but you may make more sales if you stop trying to sell

Language Focus   Keywords: *sales, decision, demand*
Fixed expressions and sentence starters for *presentations*
Business grammar: *question starters*

Discussion Topics   Describing products and services in terms of consumer benefits, decision-making skills, the customer is always right

Fluency Work   *Sales Presentations:* adopting a hard or soft sell approach to the selling of a product, service or idea

Page 81   **Unit 10: Cultural Awareness**

Text   *Boardroom Culture Clash:* the advantages and disadvantages of doing business across cultural frontiers

Language Focus   Word partnerships in the context of *meetings*
Multi-word adjectives
Business grammar: *the grammar of meetings*

Discussion Topics   The purpose of meetings, company priorities, doing business with native and non-native speakers of English, cultural misunderstandings

Fluency Work   *The Cultural Awareness Game:* two very different cultures clash in an emergency meeting

Page 89   **Unit 11: Quality Control**

Text   *Made in Japan:* Japanese manufacturing companies owe much of their phenomenal success to Western ideas which don't seem to work in the West

Language Focus   Keywords: *product, industry, manufacture*
Word partnerships in the context of *production*
Fixed expressions with *point*

Discussion Topics   Setting up production plants abroad, industrial disputes, the product life cycle, joint ventures and strategic alliances

Fluency Work   *A Question of Quality:* a current or past quality problem is presented and possible solutions are discussed

Page 97   **Unit 12: Management Styles**

Text   *She's the Boss:* the world's corporations are still dominated by men, but more and more successful entrepreneurs are turning out to be women

Language Focus   Keyword: *company*
Word partnerships in the context of *career*
Negative adjectival prefixes *un-, in-, im-, ir-, dis-*
Business grammar: *prepositional phrases*

Discussion Topics   Male and female management styles, executive types, staff appraisal and development, recruitment, headhunting

Fluency Work   *Discrimination:* four recruitment dilemmas where practical considerations and prejudice both play a part, follow-up letter of rejection

CONTENTS

Page 105   Unit 13: Working from Home

Text   *Telecommuting:* how the executives of the future may actually be spending more time at home than in the office

Language Focus   Keywords: *work, motivate, employ*
Multi-word adjectives
Common adjective-noun word partnerships
Business grammar: *predictions*

Discussion Topics   Motivation, job mobility, career changes and retraining programmes

Fluency Work   *Are You a Workaholic?:* a lighthearted questionnaire
Looking Ahead: giving a short presentation on the future of your company and how this may affect your career

Page 113   Unit 14: Environmental Ethics

Text   *Managing the Planet:* big business is responsible for most of the world's environmental damage, but, ironically, only big business can reverse it

Language Focus   Word partnerships in the context of *the environment*
Adjectival word partnerships
Business grammar: *attitude verbs (modals)*

Discussion Topics   The environmental problems of your own country, big business and the environment

Fluency Work   *Business Ethics:* five case studies explore the commercial and ethical issues involved in running a large multinational

Page 121   Unit 15: Finance and Credit

Text   *Credit Out of Control:* bad debt has now reached epidemic proportions in the business sector and modern technology is actually making the situation worse

Language Focus   Keywords: *money, order*
Word partnerships in the context of *credit* and *debt*
Prepositional expressions about *payment*

Discussion Topics   Cross-border trade, dealing with foreign suppliers and customers, the credit card culture

Fluency Work   *Getting Tough:* a meeting of the finance department to decide whose debt to call in, a follow-up letter and phone call

Page 129   Unit 16: Economic Issues

Text   *The Death of Economics:* the greatest threat to the multi-trillion dollar world economy is the growing number of long-term unemployed

Language Focus   Word partnerships in the context of *economics* and *current affairs*
Word grammar: meanings of *common prefixes*
Business grammar: *tense review*

Discussion Topics   Economic growth and decline, political views and personal beliefs, honesty in politics

Fluency Work   *Election Campaign:* opposing political parties take part in a hard-fought election campaign – the future of a developing country is at stake

Page 137   Answer Key

BEFORE UNIT ONE

The Power of Reading

Reading is one of the best ways of developing your English. The articles in this book have been carefully written to contain the essential business language you need. Although they contain only 12,000 words, you would have to read an enormous number of newspapers and magazines to find as much useful business English. The articles in Business Matters are written to provide a concentration of really useful business English.

Identifying the Language

As you read, it is important to identify and record the language which is most relevant to you. Many of the activities in this book train you to do this. Make sure you recognize the following types of language.

1. Words and Phrases

Business Matters contains words and phrases which will be new to you and which you may want to learn:

downsize	**as a rule**
margin	**on the whole**
incentive	**in effect**

Don't try to learn every new word you meet. Not all new words you meet will be useful to you. Choose the words you plan to learn. Do you already do this?

2. Word Partnerships

Much more important than lots of new words is learning how to combine the words you already know into word partnerships. Learning business English is learning the word partnerships of business.
You must already know the three words: *market*, *into*, and *break*.
But do you know the much more useful:
 break into the market?
There is no point in knowing the word *market* unless you know the words you need to talk about markets. The same is true for all the most common business words – *product, sales, demand, price, money* etc.

Here are some more examples of word partnerships:

> **launch a product**
> **sales prospects**
> **meet demand**
> **raise money**
> **enter foreign markets**

The more word partnerships you know, the more fluent you will become and the less you will have to worry about grammar! *European sales prospects* is not only much better English than *The possibility of selling our products in Europe*, it is much simpler too!
Can you match these six common words to make two word partnerships each containing three words:

management	down	slim
out	carry	research

You will learn many powerful word partnerships in Business Matters. They are much more useful than single 'new words'.

3. Fixed Expressions

There are many expressions which are fixed – they never change. You should learn them as if they were single words. For example:

> **It can't be done.**
> **You can say that again.**
> **Funnily enough . . .**
> **As a matter of fact . . .**

Many common expressions are a lot more fixed than we think. Learning them can be a very efficient way of improving your English. Try to learn them in context: for example, disagreement expressions, clarification expressions, etc.
Many of the activities in the Language Focus pages deliberately contain many phrases and sentences which are fixed or nearly fixed. This means that you can use a lot of that language yourself immediately. Don't forget how useful learning something by heart can be.

This is Business English

Business English is a combination of the words, word partnerships, and fixed expressions which are used in business life. Business Matters brings all this language together and places it at the centre of your learning.

Global Marketing

Logo Image

A logo is the symbol by which we know a company, but what makes a successful logo – one which will be instantly recognized all over the world?

Look at the well-known logos on this page. To what do you think they owe their special appeal and memorability?

- simplicity

- symbolic design

- geometric shape

- style of lettering

- non-verbal impact

How visually memorable are logos? For example, can you remember what colour the ones on this page are?

What does your own company's logo look like? How does a powerful logo help to build up the image of a product or service in the mind of the customer?

What is 'global image'? What do you understand by the term 'the globalization of markets'?

Compare your ideas with those expressed in the article, *Going Global*.

GOING GLOBAL

Are we at the mercy of the global advertisers? This article explores some of the issues facing each one of us every day wherever we live.

Perhaps the biggest challenge now facing the international advertising industry is that of establishing 'world brands' by appealing to the global consumer in all of us. For whilst there will always be national and niche markets which require specific marketing strategies, global operations call for global campaigns. Professor Theodore Levitt of Harvard Business School first put forward the theory of 'the globalization of markets'. But the idea that there are more similarities between cultures than differences goes back to the popular image of the 'global village'.

The best in the business

It was Coca-Cola who told us in the 70s that 'they'd like to buy the world a Coke' and British Airways who announced in the 80s that they were 'the world's favourite airline'. Their universally recognized TV and cinema advertisements invented the global advertising genre and the agencies who created their award-winning commercials are today widely regarded as the best in the business.

Simple messages

The very first global commercial Saatchi & Saatchi ran for BA featured Manhattan Island being flown across the Atlantic. As their in-flight magazine put it, "the effect was breathtaking; words were hardly needed; the pictures said it all". The commercial was screened in 29 countries and caused a sensation in the industry. Since then, 'the world's favourite airline' has become a part of the language, recognized the world over. The secret, according to BA, is that the message is straightforward, easily understood and vividly expressed.

The biggest brands

In fact, only a handful of worldwide agency networks have the capacity to take on the world's biggest brands. McCann-Erikson, who have handled amongst others Coca-Cola, Esso and Kodak, came up with 'the Martini moment'. Leo Burnett gave us the Seven-Up slogan 'it's cool to be clear' and, perhaps most famously of all, the Marlboro cowboy - a theme which has been running for over forty years.

Minimalist approach

So what is it that makes global advertising so compelling and memorable? The answer to that lies partly in reducing the message to an absolute minimum. A lot of adverts pack in too much and end up obscuring their message. The global commercial gets its message across succinctly, with great impact and an emotional intensity which belongs to the universal languages of pictures and music. The commercials reinforce the brand-image independently of any real consideration of the product. And image outsells product every time.

Costs the earth

The beauty of a good global ad is that it can be used to great effect over a period of many years and still seem fresh. Global image-making, however, is a lengthy and costly business. Bringing together the best creative talent in the advertising industry usually ends up costing the earth. And critics of global ads point out that for the majority of brands global advertising is seldom the answer. Though the world is getting smaller by the day, few companies, even multinationals, have true global status and since most 'mass-marketed' products actually sell to fewer than five per cent of the masses, it doesn't always pay to think big.

Crosschecking

Which of the following viewpoints support the opinions expressed in the article?

1. Global advertising is just a current trend.

2. Global ads are generally believed to be superior to other commercials.

3. If global advertising became more widespread, only the top three or four agencies would be left in business.

4. Showing the same commercial in several countries cuts down production costs and saves time.

5. A global advertising policy usually leads to extremely bland commercials.

6. Good global ads often rely on their non-verbal impact.

7. Global commercials have more mileage.

8. Mass marketing is actually a contradiction in terms.

Find the Expressions

Look back at the last three paragraphs in the article. Find the expressions which mean:

1. a very small number

2. with excellent results

3. costs a fortune

4. not always a good idea to do things on a large scale

Read the text again. Find:

5. three words you want to use more often.

6. three word partnerships you need, with their equivalents in your own language.

7. three longer expressions, with their equivalents in your own language.

LANGUAGE FOCUS

Word Partnerships 1

The following verbs both form strong word partnerships with the word *commercial*. Find four more in the article you have just read.

1. produce
2. devise
3. . . . .   A COMMERCIAL
4. . . . .
5. . . . .
6. . . . .

What is the difference between a commercial and an advertisement?

Word Partnerships 2

All the nouns in each list below form strong word partnerships with the words on the left, but three nouns are in the wrong list. Which three? Which list should they be in?

MARKETING	plan strategy expenditure slogan mix
ADVERTISING	budget agency forces costs campaign
MARKET	leader trend share segmentation drive

Discuss

Is there a TV commercial at the moment that you particularly like or dislike?
Is there really any evidence that adverts have the slightest effect on consumer buying behaviour?
Has an advertisement ever persuaded you to buy or put you off buying a particular product?

Word Partnerships 3

Now complete the three paragraphs below using the words from the following list:

segmentation   expenditure   mix   slogans
costs   shown   run   drive   agencies
trends   campaign   produce   leaders

The total marketing (1) . . . . includes service or product range, pricing policy, promotional methods and distribution channels, but for 'world brands' who aim to be market (2) . . . . , a large part of marketing (3) . . . . goes on television advertising. When global companies organize a marketing (4) . . . . , a concerted effort is made to promote and sell more of their products and this will often involve an expensive advertising (5) . . . .

Marketers generally tend to divide markets up into separate groups according to geographical area, income bracket and so on. This is known as market (6) . . . . But a global marketing policy will obviously take much less account of local market (7) . . . . and concentrate instead on what different markets have in common.

As global commercials are (8) . . . . on TV in many different countries, the advertising (9) . . . . tend to be high and obviously only the biggest advertising (10) . . . . can (11) . . . . commercials on such a global scale. Fortunately, global commercials like those for Marlboro cigarettes and BA can be (12) . . . . for many years without looking out of date, and advertising (13) . . . . , such as "the world's favourite airline" and "Coke is it", will always be universally recognized.

Underline all the word partnerships you can find in the paragraphs above.

LANGUAGE FOCUS

Word Partnerships 4

Complete the presentation extract below by matching the two halves of each sentence. Referring back to the article will help you.

1. First of all, let me say that we look forward to facing . . .

2. But first we have to firmly establish . . .

3. However, as you know, in global terms Britain is little more than a niche . . .

4. So the question really is: how are we going to make sure we appeal to . . .

5. Well, I think what the whole campaign requires is . . .

6. We need to be running . . .

7. What I'm saying is that we have to get . . .

8. In other words, the commercial itself should be reinforcing . . .

9. Remember, image outsells . . .

10. Now, obviously, this will mean bringing in . . .

a. . . . the consumer in our home market without making the product too British for European tastes?

b. . . . our brand in the minds of the British consumer.

c. . . . product every time.

d. . . . our brand-image with strong visuals and background music and the minimum of product information.

e. . . . a global marketing strategy.

f. . . . our message across directly and simply and in a way that will cross cultural boundaries.

g. . . . the challenge of breaking into foreign markets with this product.

h. . . . market for our kind of product and demand is always going to be much greater overseas.

i. . . . creative talent from outside, but in the long term creating a Euro-ad will actually save us money.

j. . . . commercials that will work well in Britain but which we can use again at a later stage in Europe.

Quotes

Complete the following quotations on advertising:

1. Never mind the gap in the . . . . , is there a market in the . . . . ?

2. I know half the money I spend on advertising is wasted. The trouble is I don't know . . . .

3. The best . . . . is a good product.

4. You can tell the ideals of a nation by its . . . .

5. All publicity is . . . . publicity.

Do you agree? Do you have a favourite quote of your own?

Discuss

Think of a well-known market leader.
To what do you attribute its market leadership:

- a better brand-image

- superior marketing

- superior production methods

- technological superiority

- innovative research

- something else?

Who is the market leader in your particular industry?

Word Partnerships 5

Cross out the one word in each sentence which does not fit. Some of the words appeared in the article.

1. It is a **reasonably / fairly / quite / highly** cost-effective strategy.

2. It is **comprehensively / widely / universally / generally** regarded as the best TV commercial ever.

3. It is a(n) **well / lavishly / superbly / exceptionally** produced commercial.

4. The message is **powerfully / highly / clearly / vividly** expressed.

Funny Business

What eight-letter word will complete all the following expressions? Two of them appeared in the article.

It's a	lengthy costly risky tricky shady	_ _ _ _ _ _ _ _ .

Which of the above expressions refers to:

1. something expensive?
   . . . .

2. something difficult or delicate?
   . . . .

3. something uncertain or dangerous?
   . . . .

4. something illegal?
   . . . .

5. something that takes a long time?
   . . . .

Discuss

Do you know of anything in business which was slightly risky, or even shady?
Have you ever been approached to do something in business which you felt was not acceptable?

Word Grammar

One way of forming verbs meaning to *make like this* is to add *-ize* (or *-ise*) to the end of the noun or adjective. You can make a lot of verbs in this way from words you probably already know. Complete the following. The first one has been done for you as an example.

1. to make your activities more global
   ▸ *globalize*

2. to make your activities more international
   ▸ . . . .

3. to make a private company national
   ▸ . . . .

4. to make a national company private
   ▸ . . . .

5. to make something more sensational
   ▸ . . . .

6. to make something more standard
   ▸ . . . .

7. to make something more popular
   ▸ . . . .

8. to be (too) intellectual about something
   ▸ . . . .

9. to put something into a category
   ▸ . . . .

10. to introduce computers
    ▸ . . . .

11. to make something legal
    ▸ . . . .

12. to make a (too) general statement
    ▸ . . . .

13. to make something more commercial
    ▸ . . . .

14. to make something more modern
    ▸ . . . .

15. to put something on television
    ▸ . . . .

If you come across other business words which follow this pattern, add them here.

FLUENCY WORK

Case Studies

Step back in time to consider the global marketing problems of some of the world's best-known companies. In their position, what would you have done? Give reasons for your decision.

British Petroleum

Having decided that it was time to update its global image, BP was about to embark on a comprehensive five-year modernization programme. First to go was the company logo. A creative team went away to dream up a new one and, at a cost of one million pounds, came up with the following design:

Before   After

Not surprisingly, one or two of the company directors had to look twice to spot the difference, but were assured it now reflected the new corporate dynamism without sacrificing any of the old BP reliability. It came as a surprise to some of the shareholders, however, that the cost of installing the new signs and repainting BP's 22,000 petrol stations would come out at another £170 million.

What would you have done?
    Gone ahead with the project?
    Compromised?
    Axed the project?

Reasons for your decision

PepsiCo

India is a rather hot country with a population of some 850 million people, an ideal market, one would have thought, for a multinational soft drinks company. But India's protectionist stance on the market entry of foreign companies meant that PepsiCo would have problems setting up in business there. And over the months of negotiation it became obvious that Pepsi was not going to be allowed to open bottling plants in India unless it offered the country substantial aid in its economic development.

Coca-Cola had already experienced similar resistance in India when they refused to give the fiercely guarded secret recipe of Coke to the Indians so that the drink could be manufactured there. Now the Indian government had made it clear that if they were to import PepsiCola syrup from the USA, Pepsi would have to help India export its agricultural produce in return.

What would you have done?
    Agreed to their demands?
    Compromised?
    Broken off talks?

Reasons for your decision

15

FLUENCY WORK

Rolls Royce

One of the quickest ways of destroying your global image is to give your product an unattractive name. And when it comes to brand names that sound embarrassing in translation, no one has made as many spectacular mistakes as the car industry. General Motors' Nova (*No va* means *It doesn't go* in Spanish) has, of course, become a classic. So too has the Ford Pinto – in Portuguese *pinto* is slang for a small male organ. Understandably, Brazilians weren't queuing up to become the proud owners of a Pinto.

Rolls Royce, however, with its elegantly named Silver Cloud, Silver Shadow, Silver Spirit and Silver Ghost rightly felt it was above such embarrassments. Until, that is, they realized that the German launch of the evocatively named Silver Mist was probably doomed to failure. Mist, they were informed just in time, means dung or animal excrement in German. But changing the name of a product at the last minute can be an expensive business.

What would you have done?
    Changed the name?
    Compromised?
    Left it as it was?

Reasons for your decision

Discuss

Here are some well-known brand names you could find in any large British supermarket. What do you think the products are? What image does each brand name convey?

Up-market?   Glamorous?
Humorous?   Trendy?
Teenage?   Sporty?
Hi-tech?   Classic?
Exotic?   Comforting?
Macho?   Feminine?
Middle-of-the-road?
Scientifically proven?
Natural and cruelty-free?

1. Gold Blend
2. Organics
3. Black Magic
4. Bold
5. Imperial Leather
6. Galaxy
7. Hamlet
8. Lynx
9. Reach
10. Quality Street
11. Old Spice
12. Taboo
13. Butterkist
14. Pampers
15. Kleenex
16. Start
17. Blue Nun
18. Mates
19. Eternity
20. Special Brew
21. Biactol
22. Frish
23. Dairylea
24. Sure
25. Uncle Ben's
26. Sensodyne
27. Blue Dragon
28. Timotei
29. Babycham
30. Sensor

Would these names work in your country? Would any cause offence?

Enterprise

How to make a million

Trying to make your first million? Then forget about drive, initiative and ingenuity. And don't let anyone tell you it's about putting in an 18-hour day, having a sudden stroke of genius or beating the system as you work your way to the top. For statistically speaking, your chances of making a fortune will largely depend on how fortunate you are in the first place. According to all the surveys, here are four sure-fire ways of getting rich:

1. START OFF RICH.

It's depressing but true that half of Britain's 95,000 millionaires were born into wealthy families, and so were a quarter of those who head the country's largest corporations. When you're rich already it takes a special kind of person not to get richer.

2. DO BADLY AT SCHOOL.

Richard Branson, the founder of Virgin, is the classic case, leaving school at 16 to start a mail-order record company and ending up running his own airline, publishing, broadcasting, construction and holiday empire. He's not alone. Almost two thirds of the UK's top earners finished their education early. And the studious graduate is less likely to be found staying at the Hilton Hotel than applying for a job in its kitchens.

3. LOSE A PARENT.

Amazingly, only 5% of successful entrepreneurs had both parents present throughout their childhood. Perhaps a lack of parental control gives you the toughness, resilience and independence you need to make it on your own.

4. BE BEAUTIFUL.

Silly as it sounds, good looks really do get you places, both in terms of career and marital prospects. If you are too pretty, however, people may tend to assume that you're nice but stupid and pass you over for promotion.

So what can you do if you're born poor and ugly, pass all your exams and have parents who look as though they'll make 90.....?
What do you think is the secret of success?
List your ideas. Then read the article, *Entrepreneurs*.

Entrepreneurs

Entrepreneurs come in all shapes and sizes - the dynamic, the cautious and the greedy. But all of them hold an equal fascination for us. How do they do it? What's their secret? Some of the world's biggest corporations would like to know too. For entrepreneurism is in. And these days everyone wants to be an entrepreneur.

But an entrepreneur is not what you are, it's what you become, and real entrepreneurs exist only in retrospect. At first, nobody takes them seriously. They're crackpots, dreamers, unemployables. And by the time they've finally earned the respect of the business community, they've already made it. So cancel the classes on entrepreneurship and throw out your business plan. For the road to entrepreneurial success can't be mapped out in advance. You get there one sale at a time.

In the beginning only the entrepreneur needs to see the goal, nobody else. And the goal is quite

"The ultimate risk is.....

simple: you get an idea; you identify your customer; you make a sale. Then you make another and another and another until your office in the spare bedroom has turned into the tower block in Manhattan you always wanted. Forget about marketing strategy at this stage. What you need first is a steady cashflow. Bide your time. Focus on the little things. That's how it works. Big companies are just small companies that got bigger.

Take Richard Branson, for instance. For the founder of Virgin, the first ten years were a struggle, with his company suffering some cashflow problems until as late as 1980. By then the Virgin Group was running 80 different operations, none of them making large amounts of money and some of them losing money hand over fist. Yet in 1992 Branson's music business alone sold for £560 million.

Or take Nicolas Hayek, the man who invented the Swatch and brought the Swiss watch-making industry back from the dead. Hayek took on Japanese market leaders, Seiko and Citizen, and beat them on quality and price. Today he sells 28 million Swatches a year and has built a £1.6bn company in the process. The Swatch is a 20th century icon. And, incredibly, though the price of a new one has never increased, some of the highly collectable early designs are now classed as art and fetch more than £20,000 - not bad for a plastic watch!

So what is it that makes a good entrepreneur? Clearly, not the same thing that makes a good manager. For good managers tend to come from fairly conventional backgrounds. They're the bright kids everyone knew would do well, born organizers, who rise through the ranks to reach the top of large corporations. But the budding entrepreneur is more likely to be an outsider, a troublemaker, a rebel, who drops out of college to get a job, discovers a

. not taking a risk."

flair for building companies from nothing, gets bored quickly and moves on. Most of all, they'll be a master of risk-management. For risk doesn't mean the same thing to the entrepreneur as it does to the rest of us. The king of corporate raiders, Sir James Goldsmith, sums it up best: "The ultimate risk," he says, "is not taking a risk." And that's probably how he got to be a dollar billionaire.

Information Check

Which of the following topics does the article discuss?

1. The hero-status of the entrepreneur
2. How to get rich quick
3. Goal-setting
4. Perseverance
5. Enterprising managers

Interviews

In groups, spend 10 minutes preparing a set of questions about the article to ask the other groups. Use these question starters:

1. What exactly . . .?
2. What should you . . .?
3. According to the article, how would you go about . . .?
4. What's the reason behind . . .?
5. What's wrong with . . .?
6. What problems . . .?
7. Do you happen to remember . . .?
8. In what ways . . .?
9. What's the connection . . .?
10. What do you understand by . . .?

Find the Expressions

Look back at the article. Find the words and expressions which mean:

1. popular, fashionable
2. looking back
3. mad or eccentric person
4. succeeded
5. losing money rapidly
6. revived
7. fought against
8. a classic image of the time
9. climb the corporate ladder
10. the would-be entrepreneur
11. a natural skill or talent
12. a person who launches hostile takeover bids

In the text, find:

13. three words you want to use more often.
14. three word partnerships you need with their equivalents in your own language.
15. three longer expressions with their equivalents in your own language.

LANGUAGE FOCUS

Word Grammar

Put the following entrepreneurial qualities into what you consider to be their order of importance.

To be an entrepreneur you need:

a. drive
b. intuition
c. determination
d. ingenuity
e. dynamism
f. initiative
g. dedication
h. guts
i. faith
j. the killer instinct

Which five of the above can you express by using an adjective?
To be an entrepreneur you need to be:

1. ....
2. ....
3. ....
4. ....
5. ....

Now match the other five with the definitions below:

6. To be an entrepreneur you need to have energy and motivation.
7. To be an entrepreneur you need to have courage.
8. To be an entrepreneur you need to come up with ideas and make decisions on your own.
9. To be an entrepreneur you need to be prepared to destroy your competitors if necessary.
10. To be an entrepreneur you need to believe in yourself.

Discuss

These days a lot of companies try to encourage the entrepreneurial spirit inside their organizations. They talk about the 'intrapreneur' or enterprising manager with the intuition and nerve to take their company into the 21st century. Do you think entrepreneurism can work within a corporation? Can a manager ever be an entrepreneur?

Word Partnerships 1

Without referring back to the article, put the following advice on how to become an entrepreneur into the right order by numbering the 16 parts below. The first and the last parts are in the correct order.

(1) If you want to make it to
◯ sale at a time. You will, of course, need to take many calculated
◯ the top, forget about putting in an 18-hour
◯ biggest cause of business failure. Make sure you clearly identify your
◯ established. That's not how you beat
◯ risks on the way to making
◯ cashflow. For money problems in the early years are the single
◯ target customers and settle for making one
◯ your time and focus
◯ market leaders until you're well
◯ for success, so throw out your business plan, bide
◯ strategy at this stage and should concentrate instead on achieving a steady
◯ day or carefully mapping out your career in advance. There's no simple recipe
◯ your first million, but there's no point in thinking you can take on the
◯ on the little things to begin with. You can do without a marketing
(16) the system.

LANGUAGE FOCUS

Word Partnerships 2

Do you have what it takes to be an entrepreneur? Complete the 'Entrepreneurial Indicator' below using the following words.

> plan   make   open   dealing   reliant   stamina   building   goals   cope
> taking   starter   sacrifices   thrive   handle   minded   adapting   suggestions

---

THE ENTREPRENEURIAL INDICATOR

Score yourself according to how true the statements below are for you:

		YES					NO
1.	I like to . . . . . . all my own decisions.	5	4	3	2	1	0
2.	I am a self-	5	4	3	2	1	0
3.	I am totally self-	5	4	3	2	1	0
4.	I . . . . . . on competition.	5	4	3	2	1	0
5.	I'm good at . . . . . to change.	5	4	3	2	1	0
6.	I always . . . . . . well ahead.	5	4	3	2	1	0
7.	I have a flair for . . . . . . teams.	5	4	3	2	1	0
8.	I'm quite capable of . . . . . . with complex issues.	5	4	3	2	1	0
9.	I can . . . . . . a fair amount of stress.	5	4	3	2	1	0
10.	I can . . . . . with uncertainty and ambiguity.	5	4	3	2	1	0
11.	I have the physical . . . . . . to work long hours.	5	4	3	2	1	0
12.	I am quite single- . . . . about my work.	5	4	3	2	1	0
13.	I'm no stranger to risk-	5	4	3	2	1	0
14.	I'm always . . . . . to other people's	5	4	3	2	1	0
15.	I'm prepared to make . . . . . . to achieve my	5	4	3	2	1	0

Work out your score and check it in the answer key. How did you do? Does the test above take a different view of entrepreneurial skill from the article?

Quotes...

Complete the following quotations on success:

1. Success is getting what you want. Happiness is . . . . what you . . . .

2. Success comes to those who are too . . . . to look for it.

3. Success is one . . . . inspiration and ninety-nine . . . . perspiration .

4. There are no rules to success that will work . . . . you do.

5. Many a man owes his success to his . . . . wife, and his second . . . . to his success.

Do you agree? Do you have a favourite quotation of your own?

LANGUAGE FOCUS

Business Grammar 1

Reporting verbs help you to summarize later something you heard said. Match what was actually said to the later report.

What was said

1. It's absolutely vital that we expand.
2. If you ask me, it'd be madness to expand.
3. Can we look at the possibility of expanding?
4. So, just to sum up . . .
5. Very briefly, what we plan to do is this . . .
6. Are you sure this expansion is absolutely necessary?

Report

a. She raised the issue of expansion.
b. He stressed the importance of expansion.
c. She questioned the need for expansion.
d. He outlined the proposed plans for expansion.
e. She argued that expansion would be disastrous.
f. He recapped on the main points of the plan.

Match the following ways of reporting in a similar way:

1. Actually, it's true that we've gone some way already.
2. I'm afraid I'm still not convinced.
3. OK, OK. Nobody said it was going to be easy.
4. Look, just how far have you gone with this?
5. You've done your homework, I'll grant you that.
6. I can only repeat that expansion is essential.

a. He reaffirmed his position on expansion.
b. She demanded to know how far their plans had gone.
c. He confirmed that the programme was already under way.
d. She conceded that the plan was well-researched.
e. She still doubted whether any expansion was possible.
f. He admitted that expansion would be difficult.

Look carefully at the word which follows a reporting verb: confirm *that*, doubt *whether*.

Business Grammar 2

Now report the following remarks made by the Finance Director (FD) or the Managing Director (MD). Use the language given.

1. MD: It's crucial that we form a strategic alliance with the Japanese.   (stress / importance)

2. FD: Look, what I want to know is how the project is going to be financed?   (demand / know)

3. MD: Are you certain we need to raise extra capital?   (question / need)

4. FD: OK, I grant you it's going to take an injection of cash at the outset.   (concede / injection of cash)

5. MD: Let me say again how important it is that we team up with the Japanese.   (reaffirm / position)

6. MD: OK, I'll just run through the main points.   (recap / main points)

Underline all the word partnerships you can find in the sentences above.

Business Grammar 3

In English verbs are frequently combined to make more complex expressions. To do this you need to know how to form the second verb. For example:

They **refused to buy** from us.

They **delayed buying** from us.

We **persuaded them to buy** from us.

I **recommend you buy** from us.

Complete the following sentences using the appropriate form of the second verb.

1. We can't afford . . . . (take) any risks.
2. We risk . . . . (lose) everything if we fail.
3. Everything will be OK providing we manage . . . . (get) financial backing.
4. We can't really avoid . . . . (involve) the shareholders.
5. I'd recommend . . . . (concentrate) on cashflow to begin with.
6. Would you mind . . . . (run) your eye over these figures?
7. It'll involve . . . . (sacrifice) a lot.
8. Everything appears . . . . (be) all right.
9. I tend . . . . (agree) with you.
10. We used . . . . (work) in different departments, but now we work together.
11. Are you used to . . . . (take) the initiative or do you wait to be told what to do?
12. I strongly advise you . . . . (get) professional advice.
13. Have you considered . . . . (draw) up a provisional business plan?
14. Surely you don't expect us . . . . (pay) for this ourselves!
15. If we do something about it now, it'll save us . . . . (have) to sort it out later.
16. I suggest we . . . . (meet) at eleven.
17. We stopped at 11 . . . . (have) a break.
18. Thankfully, they've stopped . . . . (send) us their damned publicity leaflets.
19. Don't forget . . . . (do) that report.
20. I'll never forget . . . . (meet) them for the first time.

Underline all the fixed expressions you think you could use yourself.

Discuss

Can you think of a time when you had to use your intuition and ingenuity to accomplish something that couldn't be worked out logically?

Business Grammar 4

Now try these. You'll need to decide the connecting preposition and use the correct form of the verb.

1. Actually, I'm thinking . . . . the company. (leave)
2. Thank you . . . . to meet us at such short notice. (agree)
3. Fortunately, we succeeded . . . . the deadline. (meet)
4. I don't believe . . . . too much notice of our competitors. (take)
5. Let's just concentrate . . . . what we do best. (do)
6. I don't blame him . . . . up on his own. (start)
7. I won't prevent you . . . . ahead if you want to. (go)
8. I warned you . . . . on too much work too quickly. (take)
9. Success depends . . . . in the right place at the right time. (be)

Underline the whole verb phrase in each example.

Discuss

Do you attribute any of your own success to being in the right place at the right time?

Business Venture

How would you like to launch your own business? Your objective is to come up with a good idea for a new small enterprise and to persuade the other members of your study group (your financial backers) that your venture is the most likely to succeed. You can capitalize on your own professional experience or go for a totally new departure. It's up to you.

Step 1

Working in small groups, draw up a provisional business plan to present to the rest of your class. You may find the checklist helpful when organizing the relevant information. Do not worry about detailed cashflow forecasts at this stage, but try to anticipate any questions you may be asked about your business venture.

Step 2

When the other groups present their business plans you should use your list of anticipated questions to ask them to give further details, back up their proposals or explain anything which is unclear.

Step 3

Hold a short meeting with the rest of your class to decide on which business venture will get the financial backing. Put this to a vote. Obviously, you may not vote for your own idea, but should choose what you consider to be the best idea after your own.

BUSINESS PLAN CHECKLIST

The Nature & Objectives of the Business

- What will be your main business activity?
- What is your own professional background?
- Roughly how will the business be structured?
- Do you have an overall vision for the company?

Personnel

- Approximately how many people will the company employ and in what capacity?

The Product/Service in Relation to the Market

- What is the state of the market? Growing, static, seasonal?
- How will your products/services be positioned? Up- or downmarket?
- Who will be your target customers?
- Who will be your major competitors?
- How will you market your products or services? Trade press? Mass media? Word of mouth?

Premises

- Where will the company be located? Why?
- What kind of property will you require? Offices, factories? Leased or purchased?

Equipment Required

- What general trading equipment, if any, will you require? Vehicles, computer hardware?
- What manufacturing equipment, if any, will you require? Machinery, tools?

Sales Forecasts

- What are your sales targets for year one?
- What kind of distribution network, if any, will you require?

Financial Profile

- Roughly how much in the way of funds will you need?

Monopolies

A Girl's Best Friend?

Like classic cars, vintage champagne and 24-carat gold, there is always a market for cut diamonds. But what's so special about diamonds and why are they so expensive?

Have you ever bought anyone a diamond as a present? How do you know if it was worth what you paid for it? For in the world of diamond dealing nothing is quite what it seems ....

Try the quiz below and then check your answers in the article, *Diamonds Are Forever*. The workers pictured below are diamond miners.

1. How many companies control the world diamond market?
   a. Hundreds.
   b. A dozen.
   c. Three.
   d. One.

2. How rare are diamonds?
   a. Extremely rare.
   b. Rare.
   c. Fairly rare.
   d. Not rare at all.

3. How valuable are diamonds?
   a. Priceless.
   b. Extremely valuable.
   c. Less valuable than people think.
   d. Almost worthless.

4. Are diamonds a good investment?
   a. Yes, they always appreciate in value.
   b. It depends on the state of the economy.
   c. They always hold their value.
   d. No, you never get your money back on a diamond.

Artificially high prices

The high price of diamonds is a triumph of the commercial clout and marketing genius of De Beers, the South African conglomerate that has an 80% stake in world diamond supply. By strictly regulating the mining and distribution of diamonds, De Beers has managed to keep prices artificially high. And by turning the diamond into a universal symbol of romance it has prevented secondhand diamonds from flooding the market and forcing prices down. Even in times of hardship people are reluctant to part with their diamonds. De Beers knows that if they ever did part with them, the market would be saturated overnight.

Supply outstrips demand

World supply of diamonds has consistently outstripped demand, so logically diamonds should be cheap. If not for De Beers, the world's greatest cartel, they would be. But such has been the power of De Beers that even a glut of diamonds, massive stockpiling, chronic cashflow problems and political uncertainty have been unable to loosen its stranglehold on the $60 billion world diamond market.

Diamonds are

Invented by one of the richest companies in the world, *Diamonds are Forever* is a slogan which does not bear close examination.

Common and untradeable

Diamonds are neither valuable nor rare. Though fabulously expensive, they are actually one of the most common minerals on earth. In the West cut diamonds outnumber cars. They are almost untradeable as a commodity. Their resale value is significantly lower than their original cost, and nowadays they can easily be substituted in all their industrial uses. In fact, without the tradition and romance which have always given diamonds their sentimental value, they would be almost worthless.

Cheap labour

Most of the diamonds traded internationally are mined by the African poor or bought on the cheap from the Russians. And three quarters of the world's gems are cut in poverty-stricken Surat in India, often by young children earning as little as four American cents per stone. Appalled by De Beers' business ethics, America outlawed the company, effectively preventing it from opening its own outlets in the United States. Ironically, America remains by far De Beers' single biggest market and the company operates through American dealers unhindered.

Engagement Rings

It was the marketing magic of De Beers which persuaded Americans at the turn of the century to adopt the European custom of giving a diamond engagement ring as a token of marriage. The same magic worked again in the 1950s when the Japanese in their desire to be Western became the world's second largest market for cut diamonds. And when the Oppenheimer family, who own De Beers, found themselves with a mountain of unsold small diamonds on their hands, they dreamt up the idea of the eternity ring as a means of getting rid of them.

Successful advertising
A perfect example of a near total monopoly, De Beers has always found ways to boost demand and cut surplus production. When General Electric discovered a way to produce high-grade synthetic diamonds, De Beers still managed somehow to prevent GE undercutting their prices. In fact, the Oppenheimers have spent more than $160 million a year repeating their message that "diamonds are forever", probably the most successful advertising slogan of all time. And even when profits are down and their share price takes a tumble, De Beers makes sure that the legend of the diamond lives on.

Forever

Massive stockpiling
Yet throughout its long and chequered history, what De Beers has feared most is the prospect of plunging prices if other diamond producers were ever to dump their surplus gems onto the world market. After all, it was by threatening to do just that that the Oppenheimers were able to seize control of De Beers in the first place. So far the company has managed to soak up excess supply by buying up most of the diamonds in the world. But this has led to a massive accumulation of stocks in South Africa with perhaps a further ten billion dollars worth in Russia alone. How long De Beers can contain such a huge surplus is now open to question and perhaps even they will eventually fall victim to the relentless laws of supply and demand.

Response

What is your immediate reaction to the information given in the article?
Tick the response nearest to your own.

1. I'm amazed.
2. I'm appalled.
3. I don't believe it.
4. I think it's a bit biased.
5. It doesn't really surprise me.
6. Actually, I knew about it already.

Find the Expressions

Look back at the article.
Find the expressions which mean:

1. to moderate the extent of its control
2. a sharp decline in the value of its stock
3. the varied fortunes of the past

Information Check

In groups, spend 10 minutes preparing a set of questions about the article to ask the other groups. Use these question starters:

1. Why is it that...?
2. What would you say was...?
3. What are the implications of...?
4. What precisely...?
5. What are the chances of...?
6. What do you understand by...?
7. According to the article...?
8. How might...?

The State of the Market

Study the diagram below for a few minutes. Concentrate on the terms you have not heard before. Work out the meaning of any new words and expressions from the pictures.

Now match the expressions to the following meanings:
1. start competing in the market
2. be prevented from competing
3. the market is bigger than it used to be
4. the market is smaller than it used to be
5. the market is in a good state
6. the market is in a bad state
7. supply exceeds demand
8. describes a sudden process
9. describes a gradual process

Market Expressions

Now complete the following presentation extract.

The US market was fairly 1. . . . . when we finally managed to 2. . . . . it three years ago, even though it was largely 3. . . . . by two or three big American players. And over the next two years both the market itself and our market share 4. . . . . significantly. Since then, as you know, much cheaper products from East Asia of almost equal quality to our own have 5. . . . . the market. At first the main threat came from Korea, but now it looks as though Taiwan is set to 6. . . . . the market too. I'm sure I do not need to tell you that if this trend continues the US market will become completely 7. . . . . and may even 8. . . . . altogether.

I'm afraid the picture in Western Europe is not much better. European trade disputes have further 9. . . . . a market which was already 10. . . . . from the effects of the recession.

The one piece of good news, however, is that going into Central Europe turned out to be the best move we have made for some time. We 11. . . . . that market in October. At first, it looked as if the competition in Poland and the Czech Republic would 12. . . . . us out of the market before we could establish ourselves, but fortunately that did not happen. And, in spite of currency difficulties, I can assure you that that market at least remains buoyant.

Presenting

Read the presentation above aloud, as if **you** were giving the presentation. Read it several times until you feel it sounds clear, positive, and effective.

Opposites

Find six pairs of opposites in the following words relating to trade. Not all of them appeared in the article.

1. surplus
2. boom
3. stockpiling
4. disaster
5. failure
6. prosperity

a. dumping
b. hardship
c. triumph
d. shortage
e. slump
f. success

Complete the following using some of the words above:

In times of 7. . . . . when there is very little money about, for example during an economic 8. . . . . , people often stop buying all but the essentials. This then leads to one 9. . . . . after another as companies find it more and more difficult to sell their products.

10. . . . . becomes unavoidable as warehouses fill up with unsold goods, and some companies may be forced to engage in 11. . . . . , the unfair practice of selling goods at ridiculously low prices in overseas markets. These markets are then likely to suffer a 12. . . . . of goods themselves, pushing their prices down further and destroying the conditions for fair trading which create long-term 13. . . . .

Underline all the word partnerships you can find in the text above.

Word Grammar 1

All the following verbs except one can be prefixed by both *under-* (meaning *to do this too little or too low*) and *over-* (meaning *to do this too much or too highly*).

Which one is the exception? Does it match with *over-* or *under-*? What does it mean?

-estimate   -rate   -value   -react
-state   -cut   -charge   -price

Which of the verbs:

a. are concerned with money?
b. are concerned with opinions or attitudes?

Look in your English-English dictionary for other words which begin *under-* or *over-* which you think will be useful.

Discuss

How are companies affected by economic recession and boom? How do they respond to sudden rises and falls in demand?

To what extent does your company influence or follow the market? Have you ever been involved in a trade war?

LANGUAGE FOCUS

Word Grammar 2

Complete the following by using the correct form of the verbs below. Use each verb once only. Not all of them appeared in the article.

outsell	outclass
outbid	outnumber

outstrip	outmanoeuvre
outperform	outrank

1. In the West cut diamonds . . . . cars.

2. Sales may be up, but are we actually . . . . our main competitors? That's what I want to know.

3. Both companies wanted to buy us out, but in the end the Saudis . . . . the Americans.

4. When it came to actually manufacturing the product, we were totally . . . . by the Koreans.

5. World supply of diamonds has consistently . . . . demand.

6. As a supplier and distributor of diamonds De Beers . . . . all other companies.

7. We lost the negotiation because we were completely . . . . in the final stages.

8. In terms of ease of use, speed and efficiency, it . . . . all similar products.

What is the meaning of the prefix *out-* in the verbs above?

Word Partnerships

Now match the following words and phrases to make complete expressions from the article. The first one has been done for you as an example.

1.	world	cashflow	cartel
2.	world's	diamond	of stocks
3.	chronic	accumulation	problems
4.	massive	greatest	supply

5.	keep	surplus	artificially high
6.	saturate	prices	production
7.	cut	a huge	overnight
8.	contain	the market	surplus

9.	force	surplus gems	of a company
10.	dump	control	supply
11.	seize	excess	down
12.	soak up	prices	onto the market

Discuss

Is there really such a thing as a free market? How might the activities of monopolies and cartels be restricted? Is the market you operate in dominated by one or two big companies?

FLUENCY WORK

Group Discussion

Work with a partner. Prepare to answer questions on the state of the market you operate in and the current market position of the company you work for.

	MY COMPANY	MY PARTNER'S CO.
Name of company		
Product/Service		
Approx. size of world market		
Main customers		
Approx. market share		
Main competitors		
General market trend		
Reasons for trend		

Press Conference

Work in two groups: representatives of the De Beers company and members of the Press. Prepare to hold a 20-minute press conference at which De Beers will answer questions on its business practices and company policy.

Representatives of De Beers – turn to the next page.
Representatives of the Press – read the information on this page.

Asking tough questions

Isn't it true that . . . ?
How can you justify . . . ?
Do you deny . . . ?
Do you or do you not . . . ?
Please just answer the question.
Do you expect us to believe that?

THE PRESS - Information

Re-read the article, *Diamonds Are Forever*. As a group prepare to question the representatives of De Beers about their business activities. You might mention the following:

● Isn't the high price of diamonds simply a result of De Beers' manipulation of the world market?

● If the cutting of diamonds is such a skilled and expensive business, how come 75% of the world's diamonds are cut by workers in India who are so badly paid?

● How can De Beers justify its monopolistic control of the world diamond market when diamonds are produced in so many different parts of the world?

● Aren't the advertisements De Beers runs misleading to say the least? And isn't it about time they admitted how common diamonds actually are?

● How does De Beers plan to contain the recent flood of Russian diamonds onto the market?

● Is there any truth in the rumour that De Beers has in the past dumped surplus stocks of diamonds in the sea to keep prices up?

DE BEERS - Information

Re-read the article, *Diamonds Are Forever*. As a group prepare to answer any questions the Press might ask. The following might be useful:

● The fact that there are many diamond deposits in the world does not mean that the beautifully cut and polished gems people buy are not rare. It's the processing of the diamonds that raises their value and price.

● In a free market economy you don't see anything wrong in running a highly successful advertising campaign to promote the status-symbol image of diamonds. Surely no one can be in any doubt that they are beautiful and desirable gems. If the advertisements were at all dishonest, the Advertising Standards Authority would have insisted they were withdrawn.

● As a matter of fact, the retail market for diamonds is looking buoyant at the moment and demand shows no sign of falling off. But reports that Russia may flood the market are alarming.

● As the demand for industrial diamonds continues to decline, it may be necessary to scale down production until stocks are sufficiently reduced. But this is just good business.

● Remember that many Third World countries depend on De Beers' expertise in the diamond industry to provide them with suitable outlets for their gems. They wouldn't come to De Beers if De Beers didn't offer them the best deal.

Defending your position

I'm afraid, it's not as simple as that.
With respect, you don't seem to understand
If I could just finish what I was saying.
We utterly deny that . . .
I can only repeat what I've already said, namely that . . .

Letter to the Press

As the Director of Public Relations for your company, write a letter to one of the leading business publications complaining about the misleading report on your company's business practices, which featured in the 'Focus' column of their magazine. You may find the notes below helpful.

What you'd like to say...

You swine!
    I was absolutely furious when I read the vicious report in your Focus column on Dec 7 about the way we run our company. When I gave up an hour of my precious time to speak to your wretched reporters I never thought they were going to do such a demolition job on us. Let me tell you that practically everything your article says is wrong and I've listed a number of points you made which I consider to be nothing less than downright lies! Your article makes us look like a bunch of crooks and could ruin sales, so you'd better print a retraction. At the very least, I expect this letter to appear in the letters column of the next edition of your disgraceful journal! I can't wait to hear what you've got to say for yourself.

Yours in fury

Notes

Dear Editor,
    Most disappointed / read / report / 'Focus' column / Dec 7 concerning our business practices / When I agreed / speak / your reporters / never expected / misrepresented in this way.
    Several inaccuracies / article / would like / draw your attention / and / enclose with this letter / itemized list / factual errors.
    Since/ article / presents our company / unfavourable light / and / matter / considerable public concern / hope / seriously consider / printing / full retraction. Failing that / insist / publish this letter / next edition.
    I look forward / hearing / your reaction.

Yours faithfully

Corporate Structure

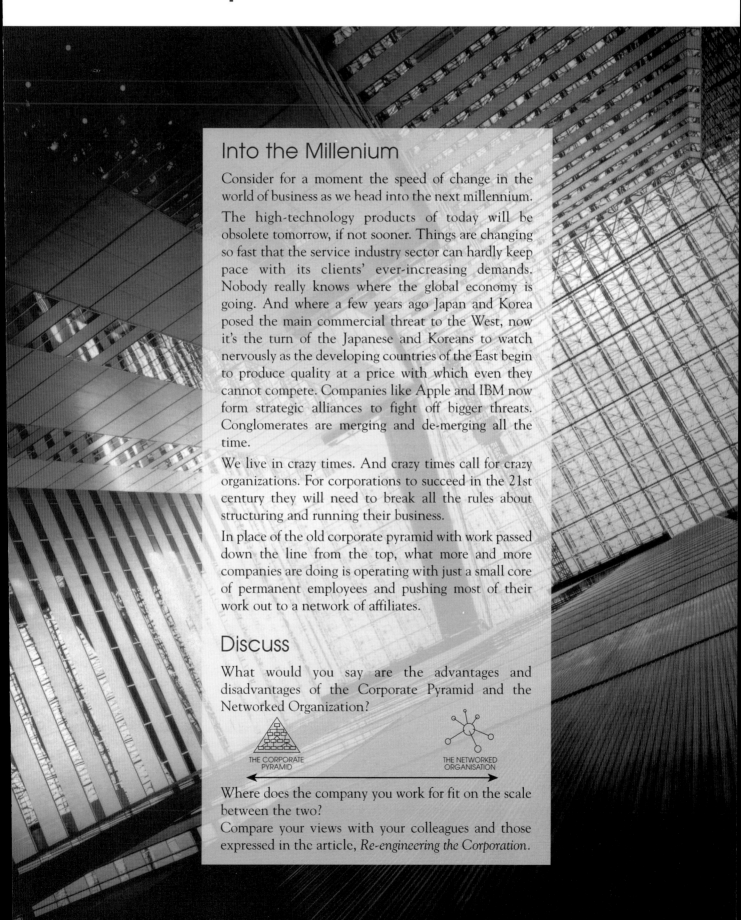

Into the Millenium

Consider for a moment the speed of change in the world of business as we head into the next millennium.

The high-technology products of today will be obsolete tomorrow, if not sooner. Things are changing so fast that the service industry sector can hardly keep pace with its clients' ever-increasing demands. Nobody really knows where the global economy is going. And where a few years ago Japan and Korea posed the main commercial threat to the West, now it's the turn of the Japanese and Koreans to watch nervously as the developing countries of the East begin to produce quality at a price with which even they cannot compete. Companies like Apple and IBM now form strategic alliances to fight off bigger threats. Conglomerates are merging and de-merging all the time.

We live in crazy times. And crazy times call for crazy organizations. For corporations to succeed in the 21st century they will need to break all the rules about structuring and running their business.

In place of the old corporate pyramid with work passed down the line from the top, what more and more companies are doing is operating with just a small core of permanent employees and pushing most of their work out to a network of affiliates.

Discuss

What would you say are the advantages and disadvantages of the Corporate Pyramid and the Networked Organization?

THE CORPORATE
PYRAMID

THE NETWORKED
ORGANISATION

Where does the company you work for fit on the scale between the two?

Compare your views with your colleagues and those expressed in the article, *Re-engineering the Corporation*.

RE-ENGINEERING THE CORPORATION

"It's not called redundancy these days . . . It's called downsizing"

If you want to stay in step with the latest management trend, fire half your staff. That's the advice of Michael Hammer and James Champy in their best-selling book 'Re-engineering the Corporation'. For Business Process Re-engineering or BPR is about smashing up the corporate hierarchies we're used to and rebuilding them from scratch. And the result is that tens of thousands of managers are losing their jobs in the name of re-inventing the corporation. In fact, some say that, if BPR really caught on, 25 million Americans would be made redundant tomorrow. Of course, it's not called redundancy these days. It's called downsizing. But it means the same thing to an out-of-work executive.

Out with vertical hierarchy

According to Tom Peters, a management guru who's clearly more excited about BPR than the 25 million looking at impending unemployment, what a lot of large companies are learning is that they can do better with four layers of management than with twelve. The vertical hierarchy is out. The new, streamlined 'horizontal network' is in. And gone are the days of the autocratic kings of industry - the Lee Iaccocas and John Sculleys of this world - for now the customer is king.

From the bottom up

Basically, BPR is a mixture of Japanese lean, flexible, 'just in time' production and American enthusiasm for re-structuring companies from the bottom up. What it means is that, in order to remain competitive, we'll all have to forget the old bureaucratic empires, divided by function into separate departments such as sales and accounts. We'll be organizing ourselves instead around continuous business processes aimed at getting the product to the customer.

Empowerment or madness?

In fact, 're-engineers' say that by the year 2000 it'll be team-players and not leaders that businesses will chiefly be looking for. And, when it comes to decision-making, middle management may increasingly find itself by-passed altogether, as more and more responsibility is passed down the line to cross-functional teams of junior managers and shopfloor workers. For by then these will have become largely self-managing, and the corporate pyramid will be turned completely upside down. BPR enthusiasts call this 'empowerment'. Others call it madness.

Mini-companies the way ahead

But is it even that? Or is it just a sexy new name for an old idea? In Sweden, where the top 20 firms do 80% of their business abroad, companies like the manufacturing giant, ABB, have already done something remarkably similar to re-engineering by breaking up the firm into hundreds of mini-companies. IBM had the same idea when it decided to form independent mini-companies of its own and 'Big Blue' set up thirteen little 'Baby Blues'. But, whereas ABB has managed to halve the development time of its products, IBM has not been able to keep pace with its smaller, fitter competitors.

The customer comes first

For BPR does seem to work better in some countries than in others. In the fast-growing economies of East Asia and Latin America, for example, it's doing well. But things don't look quite so good in the USA, and in Central Europe it's even worse. Paternalistic German bosses, in particular, find it hard to delegate responsibility to subordinates and yet overpaid German workers cost their companies 50% more than the average American costs theirs. Many French executives, too, still find it difficult to accept that the customer comes first. And in recession-battered Britain BPR is, more often than not, just an excuse to cut back and get rid of unwanted staff. Perhaps they should be getting rid of BPR instead.

Response

What is your immediate reaction to the article? Tick the response nearest to your own or sum up what you think in a single sentence.

1. I think it paints a rather negative picture.
2. I think it oversimplifies the issue.
3. I think it's a bit one-sided.
4. I think it makes some interesting points.
5. I think it argues its case extremely well.
6. I think . . . . .

Recall

Without referring back to the article, how much can you remember about:

1. mass redundancies
2. the managerial ladder
3. the customer
4. teamwork
5. mini-companies
6. cultural attitudes

Find the Expressions

Find the expressions in the article which mean:

1. the latest 'fashion'
2. right from the beginning
3. became popular
4. unemployed executive
5. management expert
6. completely restructure at all levels
7. may be excluded
8. can't match the competition
9. to economize

Read the text again. Find:

10. three words you want to use more often.
11. three word partnerships you need, with their equivalents in your own language.
12. three longer expressions with their equivalents in your own language.

Word Partnerships 1

Re-arrange these 'word dominoes' in the right order so that each makes a strong word partnership with the one after it. The first and last 'domino' are half-blank. All the word partnerships are taken from the article.

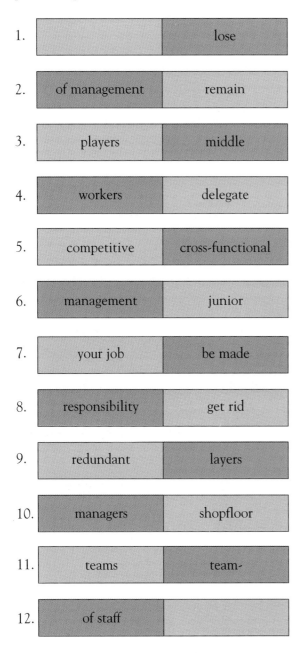

1. | | lose
2. of management | remain
3. players | middle
4. workers | delegate
5. competitive | cross-functional
6. management | junior
7. your job | be made
8. responsibility | get rid
9. redundant | layers
10. managers | shopfloor
11. teams | team-
12. of staff |

Discuss

Do you tend to work on your own initiative or do you find yourself mostly having to do what you are told?
Does your company operate specialist departments or cross-functional teams?
How many layers of management are there in your department?

Word Partnerships 2

All of the following verbs can be used to talk about the running of a company. Label each diagram with the appropriate verb. Some of the terms appeared in the article.

merge   streamline
expand   de-merge
take over   diversify
restructure   downsize

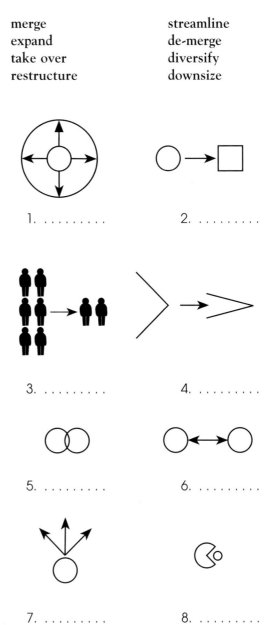

1. . . . .   2. . . . .

3. . . . .   4. . . . .

5. . . . .   6. . . . .

7. . . . .   8. . . . .

Can you make nouns from six of the verbs?

Discuss

Have you been affected by any recent changes in the structure of your company or department? Are there any mergers or acquisitions on the horizon in your industry? In major national or international companies?

LANGUAGE FOCUS

Word Partnerships 3

Complete the short dialogues below using the following phrasal verbs:

get on to   get down to
come up with   live up to
come in for   put in for
put up with   cut back on
back out of   keep up with

1. Has the restructuring of the production department speeded things up at all?

   ▸ Not really. I'm afraid it failed to . . . . expectations.

2. How's the budget for this year looking?

   ▸ I think we're going to have to . . . . spending, I'm afraid.

3. We really need to consult our legal advisors on this one.

   ▸ OK, I'll . . . . them straightaway.

4. You know, in this industry it's sometimes hard to . . . . all the latest developments.

   ▸ But that's what I'm paying you for!

5. You know, I'm sorry we ever got into this project in Hong Kong.

   ▸ Well, it's too late to . . . . it now.

6. I hear you've . . . . a promotion.

   ▸ Yes. After eight years in this place, I think it's about time they gave me my own department.

7. I think everyone's here who's supposed to be here.

   ▸ OK, let's . . . . business.

8. Look, if our team can't find a solution to this problem, no one can.

   ▸ OK, go away and see what you can . . . .

9. A lot of people were very unhappy about the way they handled the redundancies.

   ▸ I know. They've . . . . quite a lot of criticism over that.

10. If you want to stay in this job, you'll have to . . . . a fair amount of hassle, I'm afraid.

   ▸ That's OK. I'm getting fairly used to it by now.

Both speakers used a lot of useful fixed expressions. Underline all the expressions which you think you could use yourself.

Word Partnerships 4

Now, without referring back to the previous exercise, try to match up the halves of the following word partnerships as quickly as you can.

1.	come up	a.	to business
2.	cut back	b.	for a promotion
3.	get on	c.	for criticism
4.	keep up	d.	to expectations
5.	back out	e.	with a lot of hassle
6.	put in	f.	with a solution
7.	get down	g.	of an agreement
8.	come up	h.	to the accounts department
9.	come in	i.	with the latest developments
10.	put up	j.	on spending

Instead of *come up with a solution*, you can also *come up with a suggestion*. Can you find one extra word for each of the other partnerships?

Discuss

How fierce is the competition for promotion in your company? And how important is it to keep up with the latest developments? Is it better to put in for a promotion or wait for your superiors to approach you first?

LANGUAGE FOCUS

Business Grammar

Look at the diagram below. It shows the likely 'knock-on effect' at a production plant of
   a) increasing wages and
   b) freezing them at their present level.

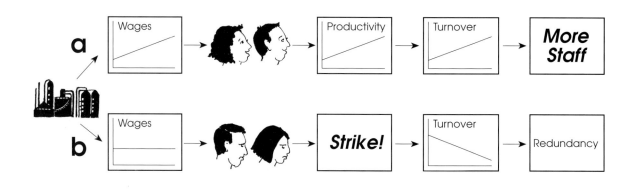

1. What'll happen if we increase wages?
   ▶ Well, if . . . .

2. What'll happen if we freeze wages?
   ▶ Well, if . . . .

3. What should happen providing the workers are satisfied?
   ▶ Well, providing . . . .

4. What might happen if the workers are dissatisfied?
   ▶ Well, if . . . .

5. What'll happen providing productivity goes up?
   ▶ Well, providing . . . .

6. What'll almost certainly happen if the workers take industrial action?
   ▶ Well, if . . . .

7. What'll we have to do if turnover doesn't rise?
   ▶ Well, if . . . .

Quotes...

Complete the following quotes on management:

1. I don't want any 'yes-men' around me. I want everyone to tell me the . . . . , even if it costs them their jobs.

2. The only thing . . . . with doing nothing is that you never know when you're finished.

3. In any organization there is always one person who really knows what's . . . . on. That person must be fired.

4. Few things are quite so embarrassing as watching your boss do something you just said . . . . be done.

5. The man who can smile when things go wrong has thought of someone he can . . . . it on.

Do you agree? Do you have a favourite quote of your own?

LANGUAGE FOCUS

Business Grammar 2

Now complete the following short dialogues by writing in the missing pair of words:

be + don't	could + got
wouldn't + were	see + tell
didn't + think	might + let
don't + be	prefer + mind
got + suggest	would + could

1. I'm going to tell them if I don't get my salary increase, I'm leaving.

    ▶ I . . . . do that if I . . . . you.

2. We're not really in a position to do anything about it just yet.

    ▶ Well, if we . . . . do something about it soon, it'll . . . . too late.

3. If we threaten industrial action, it'll give them just the excuse they've been looking for to restructure the department.

    ▶ Don't worry. We'll . . . . all right providing we . . . . push too hard.

4. We could prevent this whole mess if you'd just offer them a 2% increase on their basic wage. So why don't you?

    ▶ Look, I . . . . if I . . . . , but I can't.

5. I just don't know how to tell him he's out of a job.

    ▶ No, it . . . . be better if you . . . . me do it.

6. We've just got to economize somewhere.

    ▶ Well, unless you've . . . . a better idea, I . . . . we cut back in the training section.

7. To be honest, I don't much care if their productivity levels do drop.

    ▶ If I . . . . know better, I'd . . . . you were trying to get rid of them.

8. How are you getting on with that report I asked for?

    ▶ Actually, I . . . . do with some help, if you've . . . . a minute.

9. Would you like me to raise it at the next meeting?

    ▶ No, I'd . . . . to do it myself, if you don't . . . .

10. Where's Jack? I wanted him to give me those sales figures.

    ▶ Don't know. If I . . . . him, I'll . . . . him.

Underline all the useful expressions which you think you could use yourself.

Forecasting

Can you re-arrange the following remarks? The first word is in the right place.

1. Promotion are prospects limited fairly
    . . . .

2. We rapid envisage growth next year.
    . . . .

3. Profits tipped to are reach £600 million.
    . . . .

4. Exxon to take set looks company the over.

    . . . .

5. There's chance every of buyout a management.

    . . . .

6. There's a chance little of merger short term the in.

    . . . .

7. It the break looks as even though company might.

    . . . .

8. The are redundancies be indications that mass there'll

    . . . .

9. Employment are good prospects looking the long term in.

    . . . .

10. It good a being looks year like medium-sized for companies.

    . . . .

Which of the forecasts above seem more certain?

AeroTech: Corporate Structure

No. of board members:	8
No. of directors:	5
No. of managers:	16
No. of administrative & clerical personnel:	60
No. of production personnel:	770
No. of sales personnel:	16
No. of accounts personnel:	5
No. of R&D personnel:	4

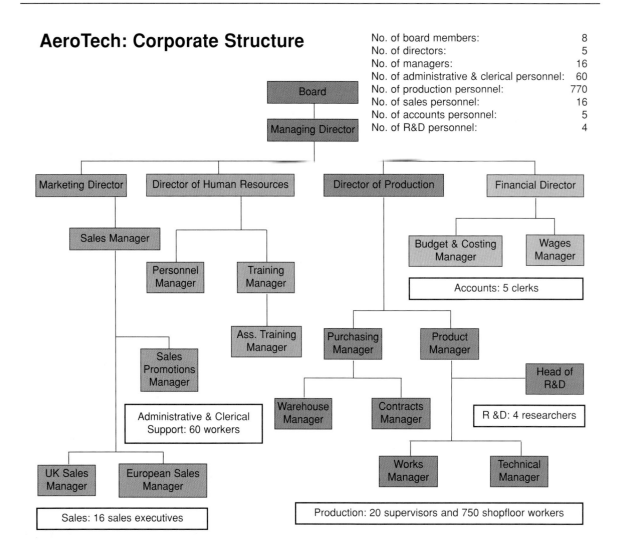

Troubleshooter

The organigram above shows the basic organizational structure of AeroTech, a medium-sized London-based engineering company, which produces electrical components for aircraft engines. Unfortunately, adverse trading conditions are hitting the company hard, and turnover has been steadily falling. The board is now insisting on a massive rationalization plan, and it's up to you to decide where the axe will fall!

Working in small groups as management consultants, decide how you think the company might be restructured to improve efficiency and competitiveness. Try to reach a consensus.

Deliver your recommendations as a short presentation of 10 minutes maximum to the management. Remember how important it is to deliver what you say in a presentation in a clear, effective, and positive way.

You might want to consider:

- whether the entire corporate pyramid should be broken up into cross-functional teams

- whether whole departments could be closed down

- whether two departments could be merged or one absorbed into another

- whether any senior and middle managers should be made redundant

- whether anyone should be promoted or transferred to another department

- which jobs could go altogether

- whether some work could be networked out to other companies or to freelancers

- whether workers need to be taken on, redeployed or laid off

Brand Management

A Follower of Fashion?

What do the following terms mean to you? Discuss them with your colleagues.

- brand loyalty
- brand-awareness
- brandstretching
- own label products
- me-tooism
- subliminal advertising
- lookalike products
- market saturation

How important to you is image? Are you very choosy about the kind of clothes you wear, the sort of car you drive, the make of watch you have? Are you as particular when it comes to the brand of coffee you drink or the type of breakfast cereal in your bowl?

Creating an Image

To find out how selective and loyal a consumer you are, try the following extract from a market research questionnaire. In each section, tick the statement you prefer, a or b.

1a. Coke and Pepsi really do taste better than other colas I've tried.

1b. One fizzy drink is pretty much the same as another to me.

2a. I wouldn't wear a cheap watch or cheap jewellery because they're a reflection of your personality.

2b. I wear a watch to tell the time and jewellery for fun. I don't care what they cost if they look all right.

3a. I wouldn't be seen dead wearing one of those Mickey Mouse fake Rolexes.

3b. I'd definitely wear a fake Rolex or Omega watch if it looked just like the real thing.

4a. I like my Audi, but if I could afford the same sort of Mercedes, I'd buy one of those instead.

4b. For me the most important thing is a car's performance and economy, not its make.

5a. I'd pay a lot more for a garment with a famous label in it because quality always shows.

5b. I'd never waste money on a silly label when you can get the same garment for half the price elsewhere.

6a. Cheap coffee tastes horrible. I don't cheat myself by saving a few pence.

6b. It all tastes the same by the time you've put three sugars in it.

7a. I only smoke Camel. I wouldn't dream of switching to another brand.*

7b. I'll smoke anything, as long as it doesn't taste of fresh air.*

* Non-smokers needn't answer this question.

Compare your answers with those of your colleagues. Then read the article, *Brand Wars*.

Brand Wars

Coke versus Pepsi; Nike versus Reebok; Nintendo versus Sega - the battle is on amongst the world's top brands.

Aggressive comparative advertising has now reached fever pitch; extra millions are pouring into R&D, and the market leaders are under constant pressure to slash their prices in a cut-throat struggle for market domination. When Philip Morris knocked 40c off a packet of Marlboro, $47-and-a-half billion was instantly wiped off the market value of America's top twenty cigarette manufacturers. Lesser brands went to the wall. And that's just one example of how fair competition within a free market has rapidly escalated into all-out brand war.

Own-Label Products

Yet, in spite of the efforts of the corporate heavyweights to win market share, when it comes to fast-moving consumer goods, more and more consumers are switching to the supermarkets' own-label products. And brand loyalty is fast becoming a thing of the past. The once unchallengeable Nescafé and Kellogg's are actually losing sales, as their higher price is no longer automatically associated with higher quality. And in many supermarkets across Europe and the States own-labels now account for over 55% of total sales. Their turnover has never been higher.

Lookalike Coke

Of course, the big brands are not giving in without a fight. When British supermarket chain, Sainsbury's, led the attack on Coke by launching its own similarly packaged product, it managed to secure 15% of the total UK cola market in just two months. But Coca-Cola was quick to respond. Sainsbury's was told to change its packaging fast or Coke would cut its prices to rival supermarkets and leave Sainsbury's hopelessly overpriced. Some people say the Sainsbury's cola tastes as good as Coke. But they're the ones who underestimate the power of the brand.

Big Brands - Big Business

For brand names are still the reason Omega can put a 300% mark-up on their watches, the reason Nestlé spent a fortune buying Perrier, the reason investors are prepared to pay up to twelve times the book value for a company's stock. Big brands remain big business in the City.

Brandstretching

Brandstretching is another way in which the household names are fighting back. By putting their familiar trademark on attractive and fashionable new products, companies can both generate additional revenue and increase brand-awareness, hence Pepsi Maxwear, Camel watches and even jewellery by Cadbury! The high-life image suits companies like Philip Morris, for whom, as the restrictions on tobacco ads get tougher, brandstretching is the perfect form of subliminal advertising.

Caveat Emptor!

So much for the high-street brands. Further upmarket, the luxury branded goods manufacturers are facing an even greater enemy of their own, namely, the pirate brands. And as the trade in lookalike products increases, companies like Ray-Ban and Reebok, Yves Saint Laurent and Armani are calling for a crackdown on the pirates, who in 1994 robbed firms of more than $10 billion in retail sales. For a fraction of the recommended retail price you can pick up fake Gucci, fake Lacoste, fake Lego, fake Disney, fake Nintendo, fake anything. But buyer beware! Your case of Moet et Chandon will probably turn out to be cider and your bottle of Calvin Klein more like industrial cleaner than perfume.

Market saturation

But, brand wars aside, the single biggest threat to the market remains saturation. For it seems there are just too many products on the shelves. In the States they call this 'product clutter' and it is currently the cause of a strong anti-consumerism movement. In fact, product proliferation and widespread me-tooism mean that some Boots stores actually stock 75 different kinds of toothbrush and 240 types of shampoo. It would take you over 20 years to try them all, assuming you even wanted to! And that's just got to be crazy when you think that 80 to 90% of new brands fail within their first six months.

Recall

Without referring back to the article, can you remember in what context the following companies were mentioned?

1. Philip Morris / Marlboro
2. Nestlé
3. Coca-Cola
4. Omega
5. Cadbury
6. Moet et Chandon
7. Calvin Klein
8. Boots

Response

Having read the article, what can you now say about the marketing terms you discussed earlier?

brand loyalty   brand-awareness
brandstretching   own label products
me-tooism   subliminal advertising
lookalike products   market saturation

Find the Expressions

Look back at the article. Find the expressions which mean:

1. has now reached a ridiculous level

2. to cut drastically

3. fiercely competitive

4. took 40c off

5. went bankrupt

6. major companies

7. total sales before costs are deducted

8. profit margin

9. pay a lot of money for

10. official value of an asset

11. extra income

12. severe measures against law-breakers

LANGUAGE FOCUS

Word Partnerships 1

Match each of the words in the first column with a word from the second column to make twelve word partnerships from the article. There are some alternative partnerships, but there is only one way to match all twelve.

1.	aggressive	a.	names
2.	household	b.	products
3.	me-	c.	advertising
4.	lookalike	d.	tooism
5.	retail	e.	goods
6.	supermarket	f.	market
7.	branded	g.	chain
8.	free	h.	sales
9.	subliminal	i.	consumerism
10.	anti-	j.	retail price
11.	fair	k.	advertising
12.	recommended	l.	competition

Discuss

Is your company a household name?
To what extent do your company's products or services rely on your name?
Are they upmarket or downmarket?
How do you differentiate them from those of your competitors?

Word Partnerships 2

The following nouns form strong word partnerships with the word *market*. Find five more in the article you have just read.

forces

penetration

MARKET . . . .

. . . .

. . . .

. . . .

. . . .

Word Partnerships 3

The following nouns form strong word partnerships with the word *brand*. Find three more in the article you have just read.

image

manager

BRAND . . . .

. . . .

. . . .

Discuss

A common criticism of target-marketing is that there are just too many identical products crowding the marketplace. Do you agree? Does your company have a problem with product proliferation?

Word Partnerships 4

Which 8-letter word can come before all the following words?

goods

research

protection

_ _ _ _ _ _ _ _   profile

advertising

durables

non-durables

Now match these word partnerships with the following definitions:

1. commercials aimed at the end-user

2. goods used shortly after purchase such as food, newspapers etc.

3. products purchased by a member of the public

4. goods which last a long time such as cars, televisions etc.

5. laws to defend buyers against unfair trading

6. market study of buyer behaviour patterns

7. description of a typical buyer according to age, sex, social status etc.

LANGUAGE FOCUS

Word Partnerships 5

Now, without referring back to the article, complete the information flowchart with appropriate words.

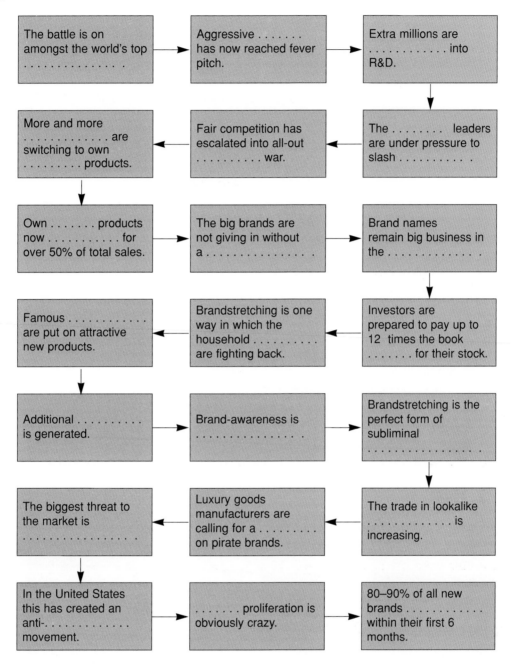

The battle is on amongst the world's top . . . .

Aggressive . . . . has now reached fever pitch.

Extra millions are . . . . into R&D.

More and more . . . . are switching to own . . . . products.

Fair competition has escalated into all-out . . . . war.

The . . . . leaders are under pressure to slash . . . .

Own . . . . products now . . . . for over 50% of total sales.

The big brands are not giving in without a . . . .

Brand names remain big business in the . . . .

Famous . . . . are put on attractive new products.

Brandstretching is one way in which the household . . . . are fighting back.

Investors are prepared to pay up to 12 times the book . . . . for their stock.

Additional . . . . is generated.

Brand-awareness is . . . .

Brandstretching is the perfect form of subliminal . . . .

The biggest threat to the market is . . . .

Luxury goods manufacturers are calling for a . . . . on pirate brands.

The trade in lookalike . . . . is increasing.

In the United States this has created an anti-. . . . . movement.

. . . . proliferation is obviously crazy.

80–90% of all new brands . . . . within their first 6 months.

Presenting

Use the completed flowchart above to give an impromptu presentation of the information contained in the article. You will need to link the main points together. If you like, give specific examples. Remember, a presentation is not an exercise in speaking correct English. Its main purpose is to inform your audience, and most importantly of all, to persuade them of what you are saying. How you say something is often as important as what you say.
Remember:
– pause slightly before important points
– stress important words
– sound interested and positive.

LANGUAGE FOCUS

Business Idioms

Not surprisingly, a lot of the language of business and marketing comes from the field of warfare and conflict. Read the following presentation and underline all the war and conflict expressions. Can you guess what they mean?

As you're no doubt well aware, we are, at the moment, in the middle of the fiercest price war we've seen for over eight years. We're under attack from all sides and in an increasingly hostile environment it's a cut-throat struggle just to survive. I'm afraid we can only rely on a certain amount of brand loyalty from our consumers and I don't need to tell you that the 'Buy British' campaign has not been entirely successful. We've lost a lot of ground to the Swiss and the Germans and have been completely out-manoeuvred by our Korean competitors. Perhaps we should be thinking of actually joining forces with the Koreans. It's a bit of a long shot, but it might just work.

Of course, with our stock value falling so sharply, we've been an easy target for the corporate raiders. But in a takeover battle it's always a question of who'll back down first and I can assure you that we'll not be giving in without a fight. For the time being, at least, we should be able to fight off the threat of a takeover.

Some of you have said that it's time to cut our losses, withdraw from markets overseas and reinforce our position in the UK instead. But I'm pretty sure that a defensive strategy like that won't work and that what we need is to take the offensive and fight back in the one market where we know we can beat the competition, namely, the United States. Our products enjoy high status in the US and, in my view, should be pushed further upmarket.

For only by taking on the competition on quality and image can we hope to win back market share.

In short, it's time to take action, ladies and gentlemen. And I propose that we re-group, change tactics and mobilize our sales forces in North and Central America. I also propose that we move towards an alliance with our main Korean competitor. And there's not a moment to lose. Otherwise, we might end up becoming yet another casualty of the recession. Any questions?

Find the Expressions

Find business idioms from the presentation to complete these definitions:

1. . . . . is when customers continue to buy a product because they have done so for some time.

2. Instead of competing in a difficult foreign market, it is sometimes better to . . . . and cooperate with a local competitor.

3. If you are making a loss in a foreign market, it is often advisable to withdraw and . . . .

4. If a particular campaign has not worked, it is best to . . . . and try a new approach.

Now complete these phrases:

5. . . . . attack from all sides

6. a cut-throat . . . .

7. lose a lot of . . . . to the competition

8. won't . . . . without a fight

9. win . . . . market share

10. a . . . . of the recession

LANGUAGE FOCUS

Business Grammar

For many companies successful marketing begins with the successful sales letter. Read through the following text on how to write the perfect sales letter. Then put one suitable word in each of the blanks.

Do you 1. . . . . stop to think about what happens 2. . . . . your sales letters after they leave your desk?
You 3. . . . . spend hours drafting and redrafting them. But do you give a moment's thought to how your reader 4. . . . . react to them when they arrive?
If 5. . . . . , don't write another word until you do.

Before you write your next letter, put 6. . . . . in the shoes of the customer. Make it reader-friendly. The majority 7. . . . . sales letters get filed, lost or binned. The reader-friendly letter stands 8. . . . . better chance.

Rule number one: never insult your reader with what is 9. . . . . a mass-mailed letter. True, mass mailing is the quickest way 10. . . . . reaching hundreds of potential customers. It's also the safest way of ensuring that your letter ends up in the bin. A short personalised letter, 11. . . . . gets to the point and clearly demonstrates 12. . . . . knowledge of the customer's needs, will invariably be better received.

As a general rule, the more important 13. . . . . person, the shorter your letter 14. . . . . be. Managing Directors are deluged with mail. They rarely have time to do 15. . . . . than glance at it and are unlikely to respond 16. . . . . your letter themselves. So in writing to MDs be brief. Junior managers, on the 17. . . . . hand, are generally looking for ideas they can pinch and present to the boss 18 . . . . their own. 19. . . . . them long and informative letters.

20. . . . . to Mark McCormack, author of 'What They Don't Teach You at Harvard Business School', different levels of management 21. . . . . responsive to different sales approaches. Senior management is usually 22. . . . . for strategic solutions to long-term problems which fit in 23. . . . . their corporate goals. Middle managers want tactical answers 24. . . . . departmental problems which will 25. . . . . their lives simpler and which they 26. . . . . easily justify to their bosses. What junior executives 27. . . . . is technical help to tackle immediate problems. Adapt your proposal accordingly.

If you've 28. . . . . three proposals to make to a customer, send three short letters 29. . . . . of one long one. It saves the reader having to wade through a lengthy document and it obviously 30. . . . . it easier to pass the proposals on to the appropriate people. Above 31. . . . . , it makes an impression. It shows style.

Some of the best sales letters don't look 32. . . . . sales letters at 33. . . . . Get someone in your research department to write 34. . . . . a memo outlining how, with your help, your prospect's company 35. . . . . be improving its business. Then send the memo on to the company explaining how you thought it might 36. . . . . of interest. Make your sales letter 37. . . . . like 'inside information' and you'll make it compulsive reading.

Remember, there's no 38. . . . . thing as a good sales letter that nobody reads. And 39. . . . . the meaning of the message is the response it gets, you can go a long 40. . . . . towards anticipating the response you'll get before you write a single word.

Underline all the word partnerships you can find in the text above.

Discuss

What do you generally do with the sales letters that arrive on your desk? Do you ever read them or do they tend to be filed in the wastepaper basket (the WPB)?

FLUENCY WORK

Product Development

Work in pairs or small groups to develop a competitive new product to challenge an established brand name.

1. Identify a household name. You should choose a product either in one of the fast-moving consumer goods markets such as food, soft drinks, alcoholic drinks, cigarettes, or cosmetics. Alternatively, choose a product from the luxury branded goods market such as perfume, watches, or fashion.

TARGET BRAND: ....

2. Investigate the popularity of the brand name. Identify three factors which contribute to the universal appeal of the product. Is it a unique product? If so, what are its special characteristics? If not, to what does it owe its popularity? Is it quality, image, availability, or price?

MAIN SELLING POINTS
1. .... 2. .... 3. ....

3. Come up with an idea for a new product to compete with the brand name. Consider the following: market positioning (upmarket or downmarket?), pricing strategy, main selling points in comparison with the brand name, packaging, advertising.

DETAILS & FEATURES:
....
....
....

NAME OF NEW PRODUCT:
....

4. Produce a consumer profile of the customer you are trying to attract. You need to take account of age, sex, socio-economic group, and lifestyle.

CONSUMER PROFILE:
....
....
....

5. Devise a simple slogan to promote the product.

SLOGAN:
....

Finally, present your idea to the others as one of these:

An R&D team – seeking the go-ahead for the new product from the board.
Sales managers – briefing your reps on the new product.
Sales reps – highlighting the features of the new product to the purchasing department of a major retail outlet.

Prices and Commodities

Value for Money

Since the only legitimate object of doing business is to make a decent profit, few things can be as important as the price tag you put on what you sell. But price is actually one of the hardest things to determine, and it's not so much a question of what a thing is worth as how much you can reasonably expect to get for it.

How do you think the general public think prices are fixed?
How would **you** define price?

- As a true reflection of value?

- Costs plus mark-up?

- Whatever the market will stand?

Which of the following points of view is nearer to your own?

"It is not the aim of this company to make more money than is prudent."
Lord Rayner, Marks and Spencer

"Pan Am takes good care of you.
Marks and Spencer love you.
At Amstrad we want your money."
Alan Sugar, founder of Amstrad.

Compare your views with those of your colleagues and those expressed in the article, *If the price is right.*

It may be true that everyone has their price, but the same can't be said of products. Products don't have a price - at least, not a fixed one. If they did, prices would not vary so much from country to country.

A personal computer wouldn't cost twice as much in the UK as it does in the States and you wouldn't need to take out a bank loan to buy a coffee in the Champs-Elysées. Of course, strictly speaking, the computer is tradeable and the coffee non-tradeable. For tradeable goods are exported all over the world, but non-tradeables have to be consumed where they are produced. And, since a refreshing café noir halfway up the Eiffel Tower can only be purchased in Paris, frankly, they can charge what they like for it. But, tradeable or not, as every salesperson knows, "The price of a thing is what it will bring." And when it comes to price, the buyer is his own worst enemy. Show me a high price and I'll show you too many customers prepared to pay over the odds.

The truth is, people pay the price they deserve. A massive 20% mark-up does not stop people buying 370 million cans of Coke a day. And with profit margins of up to a phenomenal 50%, Marlboro cigarettes can still gross nearly $40 billion a year and help make Philip Morris the most profitable company in the world.

If the price is

In fact, product-pricing lies at the very heart of the marketing process itself. Its impact is felt in sales volume, in the product's contribution to overall profits and, above all, in the strategic position the product occupies in the marketplace. For a higher price will often raise a product's profile and a high product profile commands a higher price. Product profile is basically the difference between a Rolex and a Timex, a bottle of Chanel No.5 and a bottle of Boots No.7. So, of course, is price.

But it isn't as simple as that. Economic, as well as market, forces are at work. If they were not, we might expect international competition to equalize prices everywhere, but, in spite of all the talk of a single market, a borderless Europe and a common

currency, prices remain alarmingly elastic. And what goes for a song in one country can cost a bomb in another.

For one thing, most commodities, particularly agricultural products, are usually heavily subsidized. So, in the absence of free trade, food will tend to be cheap in the USA, cheaper still in Central and South America, expensive in Europe and outrageously so in Japan. Trade barriers compound the problem. For, sadly, those who took part in the Uruguay round of GATT could barely reach general agreement on where to have lunch.

So how do you put a price on things? An everyday supermarket item in one country might be a luxury item in another and cost considerably more. Scotch, for instance, is a mass market product in Aberdeen but understandably a niche market product in Abu Dhabi. No prizes for guessing where it's cheaper.

Then, of course, there are taxes. By imposing wildly different rates of tax on otherwise homogeneous commodities like petrol, governments distort prices even further. If you're driving through Europe you'd certainly do better to fill up in Luxembourg than in Italy. Tax is also the reason why a Jaguar car costs less in Brussels than in Britain, where it was built.

So buy your car in Belgium, your fridge and

right...

other 'white goods' in the UK; stock up on medicines in France and on CDs in Germany. That way you'll be sure to get the best deal. For where you spend your money is almost as important as what you spend it on, but neither is as important as the fact that you're prepared to spend it. In the words of film actor Cary Grant, "Money talks, they say. All it ever said to me was *Goodbye*."

Recall

Without referring back to the article, how much can you remember about:

1. computers
2. Coca-Cola
3. Marlboro cigarettes
4. Rolex and Chanel
5. food
6. GATT
7. Scotch whisky
8. Jaguar cars
9. fridges
10. CDs

Find the Expressions

Find the expressions in the article which mean:

1. absolutely accurate
2. pay more for something than it's worth
3. money will get you anything

Read the text again. Find:

4. three words you want to use more often
5. three word partnerships you need, with their equivalents in your own language
6. three longer expressions, with their equivalents in your own language

LANGUAGE FOCUS

Word Partnerships 1

The following business words appeared in the article in the order in which they are listed. How many of their word partners can you find in just five minutes?

BUSINESS WORD	WORD PARTNERS
1. tradeable	
2. profit	
3. product	
4. sales	
5. overall	
6. strategic	
7. product	
8. market	
9. borderless	
10. common	
11. free	
12. trade	
13. luxury	
14. mass	
15. niche	

Choose the eight most useful word partnerships and find an equivalent for them in your own language.

Cheap or Expensive?

Sort the following into two groups. Mark those which mean expensive, E, and those which mean cheap, C.

1. It cost the earth.
2. It cost a bomb.
3. It was going for a song.
4. It cost peanuts.
5. It cost a fortune.
6. They were practically giving it away.
7. It cost an arm and a leg.
8. It was a real bargain.
9. It cost a packet.

Word Grammar

In each example use the word in CAPITALS to form another word which will fit in the space.

1. TRADE
. . . . goods are exported all over the world.

2. TRADE
China is rapidly becoming one of the world's main . . . . nations.

3. PROFIT
Unfortunately, the product didn't turn out to be very . . . .

4. PROFIT
The ratio of net profit to sales will give us an idea of the company's overall . . . .

5. PROFIT
I think we have all . . . . from a sharp increase in demand.

6. COMPETE
We've lost market share because our products are no longer . . . .

7. COMPETE
In the oil industry our main . . . . are obviously the Arabs and the Americans.

8. COMPETE
With so many similar products available already, the . . . . is very stiff.

9. PRICE
It's high time we had a thorough review of our . . . . policy before we . . . . ourselves out of the market.

10. PRICE
Some of their products are a bit . . . . We can get the same thing cheaper elsewhere.

Discuss

What is the most expensive thing you've ever bought for cash?
What's the best bargain you've ever picked up?
Have you ever been badly ripped off?

LANGUAGE FOCUS

Word Partnerships 2

All the words below form strong partnerships with the words *prices* and *price*, but the vowels are missing from each word. How many can you work out?

VERB + *price(s)*

1. c _ t
2. f _ x
3. s l _ s h
4. r _ d _ c _
5. r _ _ s _
6. q _ _ t _
7. f r _ _ z _
8. _ q _ _ l _ z _

ADJECTIVE + *price(s)*

9. f _ x _ d
10. c _ m p _ t _ t _ v _
11. r _ _ s _ n _ b l _
12. _ t t r _ c t _ v _
13. _ l _ s t _ c
14. _ n b _ _ t _ b l _

price + NOUN

15. c _ t
16. w _ r
17. r _ s _
18. r _ d _ c t _ _ n
19. s _ n s _ t _ v _ t y
20. _ l _ s t _ c _ t y
21. _ n d _ x
22. h _ k _

Word Partnerships 3

Now complete the following using some of the word partnerships above:

1. If we accept your offer, we will expect you to . . . . prices at their present level for the next 12 months.

2. If we all keep reducing our prices, we'll end up with a price . . . . on our hands.

3. You can't buy cheaper. Our prices are not just . . . . , they're . . . .

4. We more than cut our prices – we . . . . them by 35%!

5. The price of most things is pretty . . . . It depends on where you buy them and what the demand is.

6. Talk about a price . . . . ! They've practically doubled their prices every six weeks!

7. We think the price you've . . . . us is very reasonable. You've got yourself a deal.

8. Acute price . . . . has prevented us from raising our prices.

Discuss

What's the difference between mark-up and profit margin?
Roughly, what are the profit margins for the products or services you're most closely involved with?

Money Expressions

Rearrange the following to make useful business expressions. The first word is in the right place.

1. Let's figures talk.

2. Just a look figures take the at.

3. Can us you a figure rough give?

4. How these at did arrive you figures?

5. Where these did from come figures ?

6. The speak figures themselves for.

7. The encouraging not very are figures.

8. Can it you a on put figure?

Which of the above expressions mean:

a. you want an approximate figure?

b. the figures need no explanation?

Discuss

What kind of figures are the critical indicators in your own line of business?

Economic statistics?

Market figures?

Demographic trends?

LANGUAGE FOCUS

Word Partnerships 4

Now match the following words and phrases to complete these notes on the article you read earlier. Referring back to the text will help you. The first sentence has been done for you as an example.

SUBJECT	VERB	COMPLEMENT
Tradeable goods	are consumed	to pay over the odds.
Non-tradeables	are prepared	all over the world.
Too many customers	are exported	where they are produced.
People	lies	the price they deserve.
Product pricing	is felt	in sales volume and profits.
Its impact	pay	at the heart of the marketing process.
Every product	usually commands	a product's profile.
A high price	occupies	a higher price.
A high product profile	often raises	a strategic position in the marketplace.
Economic and market forces	are heavily	at work.
Prices	are also	subsidized.
Most commodities	remain	elastic.
Trade barriers	distort	on homogeneous commodities.
Different rates of tax	compound	prices even further.
Governments	are imposed	the problem.

Can you link these notes together to produce a short summary of the article? You will need extra words and phrases to connect up the facts:

but	because	for	whereas	in fact
the fact is	for example	for one thing	so, basically	by

"Whereas tradeable goods are exported all over the world, non-tradeables are consumed where they are produced. But in both cases too many customers . . . ."

Discuss

What are the main factors influencing the price of the products or services you offer? How do government taxes and subsidies affect your prices?

LANGUAGE FOCUS

Trends 1

Which graph illustrates the movement described in these sentences?

1. The market is showing some signs of growth.
2. The market is extremely volatile.
3. The pound slipped back against the dollar.
4. The Swiss franc is staging a recovery.
5. The lira lost ground slightly.
6. There's been a dramatic downturn in the market.
7. There's been an upsurge of interest in gold.
8. The share price bottomed out at 115p.
9. Sugar peaked at $400 a tonne.
10. Profits will level off at around £1.1bn.
11. Sales hit an all-time low.
12. There hasn't been much movement in the price of tin.

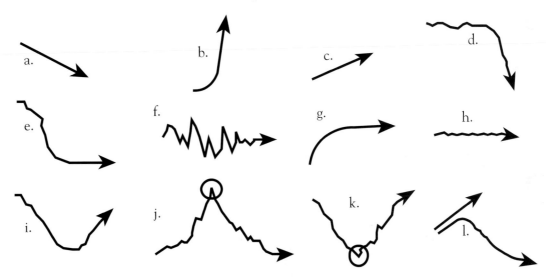

Trends 2

The financial press is full of expressions of change and development. Enter the following verbs in the chart below according to the type of change they describe:

slump	rise	recover	plunge	pick up	plummet
drop	soar	bounce back	take off	climb	rally
fluctuate	fall	stabilize	slide	flatten out	crash
hold steady	escalate	decline	rocket	dip	

1.	2.	3.	4.	5.	6.	7.

FLUENCY WORK

The Commodities Game

Of all the markets in which goods are traded the most volatile and unpredictable are the commodities markets. In theory, international commodity exchanges exist to set the standards and fix the prices of primary products, such as gold, silver, copper, tin, coffee, sugar and crude oil. In practice, the prices of some of these commodities fluctuate wildly, earning and losing speculators fortunes overnight.

Instructions

First, divide into groups of up to three. You will start off with US$1m of capital to speculate with and may buy, sell or hold any or all of the seven commodities in which you trade.

Every ten minutes

Every ten minutes your teacher* will give you an information update detailing the current commodity prices and giving you an up-to-the-minute forecast on likely changes in trading prices for each commodity. On the basis of this information you should agree on what to buy, sell or hold during this trading session. Keep a record of all your transactions. There are eight trading sessions in all.

* Teachers: The updates are on p.144.

Your objective

Your objective is to make as much money as possible by the end of the final session. You may not borrow extra capital and may therefore need to fund purchases of a commodity whose price you believe to be going up by selling your holdings in a commodity whose price you think may be about to fall. Be careful – not all the forecasts are accurate!

Beware!

Remember, 85% of all commodity speculators get wiped out. Try not to be one of them!
Look for patterns and trends in the fluctuating price of each commodity and keep track of which forecasts are the most accurate. Good luck!

TRADING SESSION	CAPITAL	GOLD $/troy oz	SILVER $/troy oz	COPPER $/tonne	TIN $/tonne	COFFEE $/tonne	SUGAR $/tonne	OIL $/barrel
Start	$1,000,000	0	0	0	0	0	0	0
CURRENT COMMODITY PRICES								
1								
CURRENT COMMODITY PRICES								
2								
CURRENT COMMODITY PRICES								
3								
CURRENT COMMODITY PRICES								
4								
CURRENT COMMODITY PRICES								
5								
CURRENT COMMODITY PRICES								
6								
CURRENT COMMODITY PRICES								
7								
CURRENT COMMODITY PRICES								
8								
TOTAL ASSETS:								

Corporate Entertaining

What's your price?

Some companies seem only too happy to spend enormous sums of money on their best clients in order to 'keep them sweet'. Does this make good business sense or is it just another form of corruption? When is a gift a bribe? And where do you draw the line?

Can you be bought? To find out how 'open to persuasion' you are, try the following test:

1. One of the suppliers tendering for a contract with your company invites you out for lunch at a top-class restaurant in London to 'talk things over'. Do you...

a. Insist that you cannot be bought and promptly scratch the supplier's name from your shortlist?

b. Politely refuse, saying that you never mix business with pleasure?

c. Take advantage of the situation by ordering a more expensive meal than you usually have?

d. Give yourself a real treat – caviar, lobster, vintage champagne, the best brandy...?

2. You have been assigned to choose a venue for your company's annual conference. The manager of one of the hotels you are considering lets it slip that there could be a week's holiday in it for you and your family. Do you...

a. Report him to his regional manager?

b. Smile and point out that free holidays are not a condition for winning the contract.

c. Gratefully accept a large en suite room with minibar and a view of the bay?

d. Ask him if he could manage a fortnight and include the use of a car?

3. The father of an applicant for a post in your company sends you a Rolex watch and a case of Bollinger champagne for Christmas. Do you...

a. Send them back with a note saying: 'Thanks, but no thanks'?

b. Return the watch, drink the champagne and forget the name of his son?

c. Give his son the job immediately and ask him if he has any other children looking for work?

d. Write him a letter saying you never received the matching Rolex he obviously intended for your partner?

There's no doubt about it, corporate entertainment is big business. In Japan, for example, where relationship-building is a fundamental part of business life, a staggering 40 billion dollars of marketing expenditure goes on corporate entertainment annually. That's roughly equivalent to the Republic of Ireland's GDP for 1993 or Venezuela's total foreign debt. The infamous Recruit Group, which has been the subject of repeated scandals in Japan, once paid fifteen-and-a-half thousand dollars for a single meal for a dozen executives at a favourite restaurant. So it's easy to see how the money the Japanese spend in a year on wining and dining important clients could add up to the cost of 365 brand-new jumbo jets!

To some, corporate entertainment is merely an expensive and perhaps unnecessary luxury. To those who take a dimmer view it's nothing short of bribery. But the truly corrupt corporate entertainer is relatively rare. Famous fraudsters, the Bank of Credit and Commerce International, did indeed specialize in 'sweetening' their most valued clients - frequently international terrorists, drug barons and Third World dictators - with shopping sprees in London and endless lines of credit at Las Vegas casinos. But this is a million miles away from an everyday business

Looking After the Twenty Percent

breakfast at the Hilton or a power lunch at the Savoy. For most successful business people would agree that goodwill is a crucial part of clinching lucrative deals and these days goodwill costs more than a smile.

A few years ago, the Ritz Hotel, recognizing the major contribution made by executive diners to its restaurant turnover, invented the award of Business Luncher of the Year to honour, in their words, "the executive who does most to help the recovery of the economy by lunching out". Only those who spent in excess of £5000 a year stood a chance of winning but there was no shortage of candidates willing to compete.

What the Ritz was acknowledging is that business lunches are an important part of corporate culture, whether to consolidate professional relationships between colleagues and charge it to expenses or to manipulate over-cautious clients into an immediate agreement. After all, it's rather difficult to reject your host's proposal (however unspeakable) when you have just eaten a hundred dollars' worth of their entertainment budget!

How cost-effective it really is for Fiat to own an art gallery so it can take customers on special conducted tours or for the German Neckerman company to have a whole department organizing weekends in the Mediterranean for important clients is, of course, open to question. Certainly in Austria, where corporate entertaining is tax-free, offering Mozart festivals to music-lovers and Klosters to corporate skiers seems to promise a good return on an initial investment. But can it legitimately be considered part of a company's overall marketing effort?

It can. What more and more companies are realizing is that across-the-board marketing doesn't work. Marketing in the future will have to be more clearly focused. And it may turn out that big above-the-line media campaigns prove less effective in moving goods than simpler strategies for getting the client on your side. Of course, in times of recession corporate hospitality looks extravagant and doesn't make for good public relations. But it still makes sense to target your best clients. For if the so-called Pareto Principle is true and eighty percent of your business really does come from twenty percent of your customers, then shouldn't you be looking after the twenty percent?

Response

1. What in the article did you personally find most amusing, interesting, surprising, and shocking?

What amused me was . . .
What interested me was . . .
What surprised me was . . .
What shocked me was . . .

2. Was there anything in the article that annoyed you or you thought was wrong?
Was there anything you didn't know?

It annoyed me that
. . . .
I wasn't aware that
. . . .
I'm not sure about
. . . .

Find the Expressions

Find the expressions in the article which mean:

1. This is certain.
2. This is a different thing altogether.
3. This is doubtful.

Expand

Without referring back to the text, can you expand on the following facts and figures mentioned in the article?

1. $35 billion
2. The Republic of Ireland and Venezuela
3. $15,500
4. 365
5. BCCI
6. The Ritz
7. Fiat and Neckerman
8. Tax
9. Above-the-line marketing
10. The Pareto Principle

LANGUAGE FOCUS

Summary

Now complete the following summary of the first half of the article using the words below. Referring back to the text will help you.

culture	scandals
part	entertainment
marketing	contribution
luxury	clients
hospitality	extravagant

A lot of people regard corporate 1. . . . . as an unnecessary 2. . . . . , but not the Japanese! As far as they are concerned, it makes a major 3. . . . . to a company's overall 4. . . . . effort, and they spend a staggering $40 billion a year looking after their most important customers. That's roughly equivalent to Ireland's GDP for 1993!
And, though there have been repeated 5. . . . . in Japan involving the most 6. . . . . companies, extending 7. . . . . to your most valued 8. . . . . remains a crucial 9. . . . . of Japanese corporate 10. . . . .

Without changing the meaning too much, which of the adjectives in the summary above could be replaced by the following:

a. significant?   c. phenomenal?

b. total?   d. vital?

Underline all the word partnerships you can find in the summary above.

Word Partnerships

Re-arrange these 'word dominoes' in the right order so that each makes a strong word partnership. The first and last domino are half-blank.

1. | | corporate |
2. | effort | public |
3. | on an investment | marketing |
4. | lunch | lunch |
5. | and dining | sweeten |
6. | out | consolidate |
7. | to expenses | a return |
8. | valued clients | power |
9. | building | wining |
10. | relationships | charge it |
11. | entertainment | relationship |
12. | relations | |

Discuss

What do you understand by the terms *above-the-line* and *below-the-line* marketing? Can corporate entertaining really be considered a below-the-line marketing strategy?

LANGUAGE FOCUS

Describing Food

Describing food and drink to someone who doesn't know much about your local cuisine is not always an easy thing to do. What noun from this list will form strong word partnerships with all the words below?

meat   salad   dish   red wine   food

meal   steak   beer   white wine   vegetables

1.   light   heavy   quick   vegetarian
2.   rich   spicy   plain   fast
3.   traditional   unusual   exotic   local
4.   roast   stewed   cold   sliced   minced
5.   rare   medium   well-done   fillet
6.   fresh   frozen   crisp   seasonal
7.   green   side   chicken   mixed
8.   light   full-bodied   robust
9.   dry   medium   sweet   crisp   fruity
10.   strong   bottled   export   draught

Discuss

Does your firm do any kind of corporate entertaining? What about corporate gifts? Have you received gifts from companies for whom you're a major client?

Which of the following gifts wouldn't you mind receiving?

- A travel clock-radio?

- Golf balls with your name on them?

- A case of red Bordeaux?

- A leather briefcase with your initials embossed in gold?

- A personalised pen set?

Which of the following gifts have you actually received?

- A cheap biro with your supplier's logo on it?

- A desk diary with adverts for your supplier running through it?

- A calendar featuring photographs of your supplier's factories?

Expressions with 'deal'

Divide the following expressions into two groups – those which mean *We reached a deal* and those which mean *We failed to reach a deal*.

1.   We clinched the deal.
2.   We wrapped up the deal.
3.   We blew the deal.
4.   We struck a deal.
5.   We swung the deal.
6.   The deal fell through.
7.   We screwed up the deal.
8.   The deal's off.

Discuss

How often do you eat out on expenses in a month? What's the most you've ever spent on wining and dining an important client? Was it worth it?

Have you ever clinched a deal over a meal? Or don't dinner and business mix?

Does 80% of your business really come from 20% of your clients or do you think that's an exaggeration?

The Business Lunch

Rearrange the following to make complete sentences. The first word is in the right place.

1. There's new a nice Italian corner just the restaurant round.

2. There's Thai pretty restaurant a good go we where usually.

3. There's popular little a very restaurant has which opened just.

4. There's restaurant nice a quite fish you like might which.

5. There's vegetarian wonderful a does excellent restaurant which an lasagne.

Discuss

What sort of food do you like? Do you have a favourite place you take people to for lunch or dinner?

Do you ever have working breakfasts? Do you have to give up many of your evenings to socializing with business contacts? If so, does this affect your home-life?

Have you ever had to attend a business meal which you really did not want to be at?

Have you ever had to pretend you were enjoying some food that you really did not like?

Spoken English

During a meal out with a client or colleague when would you expect to hear the following? Match the expression with its meaning.

1. What can I get you?
2. That sounds nice.
3. How's yours?
4. Just a drop, thanks.
5. It's an acquired taste.
6. Nothing to start with, thanks.
7. No, I'm all right thanks.
8. Don't wait for me.
9. Where's the loo here?
10. This one's on me.
11. No, no, I insist!

a. From your description, I think I'm going to like this dish.
b. Can you tell me where the toilet is?
c. No thank you. I don't want any (more).
d. I'll have just a little more wine, thank you.
e. Please start.
f. You must let me pay!
g. What would you like to drink?
h. It's unusual and you may not like it at first.
i. I'll pay.
j. What is your meal like?
k. I don't want a first course, thank you.

FLUENCY WORK

Mixing Business with Pleasure

In the space below write out part of a restaurant menu which would be typical of the city or town where you live. Two or three starters, main courses and desserts should be sufficient. Try to include a few local specialities if you can. Don't translate the names of the dishes into English – write them in your own language. Look up any extra vocabulary you'll need to describe the dishes.

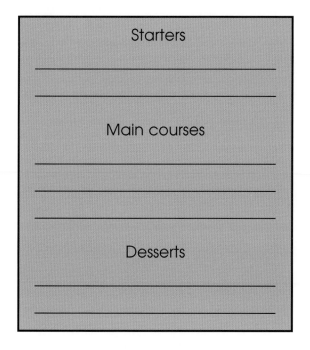

Starters

_____

_____

Main courses

_____

_____

_____

Desserts

_____

_____

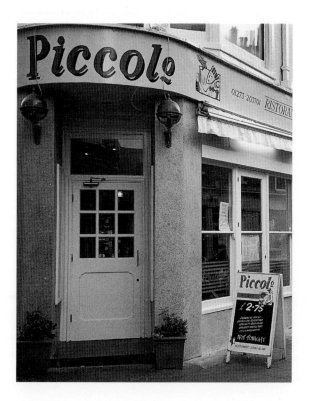

Describing Food

It's a kind of ...
It's a bit like ... only more / less ...
It's fairly / quite / rather ...
It's made from ... with ... and cooked in ...
It's served with ...
I think you'll like it.
You may not like it.

grilled	**boiled**	**roast**	**stir-fried**
poached	**stewed**	**baked**	**fried**

Business over Dinner

A supplier and client are going to have dinner. Work in pairs. Decide who is going to be the supplier and who is going to be the client in the following conversation. Here is the information for the Supplier. The information for Clients is on the next page.

The Supplier

You are in a local restaurant with a foreign client. As they don't speak your language very well, you're both speaking English.

1. Try to relax them by asking them how they like your town/city. Ask them if they'll have time to see much of it during their stay. If so, make a few recommendations as to what they might see and do. Keep the conversation going by talking a little about current affairs, sport, the weather, holidays, your family, their family (if culturally appropriate).

2. Ask them what they'd like to eat and drink, using the menu you have just created above. If necessary, try to explain some of the things on the menu. Remember to make the dishes sound appetizing and appealing.

3. Your main objective during lunch is to do some business. So, once you've established a friendly atmosphere, try to get the conversation round to the subject of the contract your company has with theirs for the supply of electrical components. You know you are not the only supplier your client uses, but you believe it would be mutually advantageous if you were. For one thing, if you had an exclusive arrangement with your client you might be able to double the discount you offer them to 11%. Be careful not to sound too pushy, but take every opportunity to talk business during the meal.

The Client

You are in a foreign restaurant with a local supplier. As you don't speak their language very well, you're both speaking English.

1. Answer your host's questions and talk about your impressions of their town/city so far. Ask them what there is to see and do in the city and remember to respond enthusiastically to some of their suggestions. If you don't like the suggestions, be diplomatic! Keep the conversation going by talking a little about current affairs, sport, the weather, holidays, your family, their family (if culturally appropriate).

2. Decide what you'd like to eat and drink. If there are things on the menu you don't

understand, you could ask your host to explain them to you. If you're not sure what to choose, perhaps your host can recommend something. Remember to sound interested in the food.

3. Your host's company is one of three which supply yours with electrical components and you are quite happy with this arrangement. You really don't want to re-negotiate your contract with them and, anyway, you don't believe in mixing business with pleasure. Without being rude, avoid getting into any discussions about business. If business does come up, try to change the subject.

Innovation

How creative are you?

Do you consider yourself to be creative? Are you the sort of person who gets sudden flashes of inspiration or are you more of a methodical problem-solver?

To find out how good you are at thinking your way around a problem, try this: connect all the circles below with the minimum number of straight lines without lifting your pen from the paper.

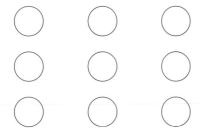

Discuss

Do you find this kind of puzzle interesting or infuriating? What sort of skill, if any, do you think it is testing?

How important is creativity in business? Are creativity and innovation the same thing?

Some suggest that luck plays a major part in any innovative breakthrough. Below is a list of tips on how to maximize your chances of striking it lucky, taken from Tom Peters' bestseller, 'Liberation Management'. Which piece of advice strikes you as:

- the most useful
- the cleverest
- the silliest

1. Listen to everyone. Ideas come from everywhere.
2. Don't listen to anyone. Trust your inner ear.
3. Constantly reorganize. Mix, match, try different combinations to shake things up.
4. Read odd stuff. Visit odd places. Make odd friends. Work with odd partners.
5. Disorganize.
6. Get out of your office.
7. Get rid of your office.
8. Nurture intuition.
9. Forget the same tired meetings, talking with the same tired people about the same tired things.
10. Get fired. If you're not pushing hard enough to get fired, you're not pushing hard enough!

Do you have a strategy of your own for coming up with new ideas?
Work in two groups. One group should read the article entitled *Bright Ideas*, the other should read the one entitled *The Lateral Thinker*.

Bright Ideas

The scene is the boardroom of a multinational cosmetics company at the end of an exhausting all-day meeting. The conference table is littered with screwed up papers and empty Perrier bottles. The financial controller is tearing his hair out and the director of R&D is no longer on speaking terms with the head of marketing. The launch of a new shampoo has backfired badly. All decisions have had to be deferred until the next meeting. Nobody even wants to think about the next meeting.

At this point a young marketing consultant cuts in. "Ladies and gentlemen, I have an idea which is guaranteed to double sales of your new shampoo. Now, believe it or not, my idea can be summed up in just one word and for $30,000 I'll tell you what it is." Naturally, objections are raised, but the chairman finally agrees to the deal. "Here is my idea. You know the instructions you put on the back of the shampoo bottle? I suggest you add one word to the end. And the word is: 'repeat'."

Not all good ideas are this simple, but in business a surprising number of them are. At least, they seem simple after they've been thought of – the secret is to think of them in the first place. As someone once remarked, "if you can't write your idea on the back of your business card, you don't have an idea".

So what are the conditions for creativity in business? And is there a blueprint for having bright ideas? Here's what the psychologists think:

1. Be a risk-taker. Those who are reluctant to take risks don't innovate.
2. Be illogical. An over-reliance on logic kills off ideas before they have a chance to develop.
3. Let yourself be stupid from time to time. Great ideas often start out as stupid ideas.
4. Regularly re-think things. Problem-solving frequently involves breaking up problems into parts and putting them back together again in a different way.
5. Take advantage of lucky breaks. The most creative people never ignore an opportunity.

They say the West creates and the East innovates, and there may be some truth in this. Take British entrepreneur, Sir Clive Sinclair, the great electronics inventor of the 70s, whose C5 electric car flopped when people found it quicker to get out and walk. Then take Akio Morita, the chairman of Sony, who has seen his company claim 85% of the world personal stereo market with the much imitated Sony Walkman – a masterly innovation which merely took advantage of existing technology. The comparison speaks for itself.

And maybe one reason high-technology companies seek to merge multinationally is so that they can combine both creative and innovative strength. For anything that won't sell isn't worth inventing and it's an expensive waste of time coming up with ideas you can't exploit. But it's even more expensive if your competitors can exploit them. And there's not much point doing the research if another company is going to end up doing the development, and making the profit.

The Lateral Thinker

In his book on creative problem-solving, 'Breaking Through', Tom Logsdon tells the story of a bright young executive hired to manage a San Francisco hotel. One of the first problems the young executive has to face is a flood of complaints about the hotel lifts, which are infuriatingly slow. Guests are actually starting to demand rooms on lower floors. But an upgrade of the lift system is ruled out when the lowest estimate for reconstruction comes to $200,000. Clearly something else has to be done, and pretty quickly, before people start checking out.

Finally, a creative solution occurs to the young executive. The key to the problem, he decides, is boredom. With only the lift doors and a blank wall to stare at, guests are understandably getting bored, and when people are bored they tend to complain. So instead of speeding up the lifts, full-length mirrors are installed both inside and directly outside the lifts on each floor – at a cost of just $4,000. Now, with their reflections to look at when they use the lift, people stop complaining, thereby saving the hotel $196,000.

This is what Edward De Bono calls lateral thinking, and it's the result of looking at the problem in a different and unusual way. Indeed, reformulating and redefining a problem is just one of the ways in which you can create a climate for creativity in business. And an increasing number of companies now see such creative strategies as vital to their survival.

At 3M, for example, employees spend as much as 15% of their time on new ideas and 25% of every manager's product portfolio consists of products that are less than five years old. At Hewlett-Packard more than half their orders in 1992 were for products introduced in the previous two years. It's a similar story at Glaxo, ICL and SmithKline Beecham. For it's no coincidence that in research-driven industries, like computers and pharmaceuticals, an innovative lead creates the market leaders. Management guru, Tom Peters, talks nowadays of a company's whole culture being creative. But creativity would be useless without innovation, and the two terms should not be confused.

According to the team running creativity courses at the Cranfield School of Management, creativity is essentially about generating, not judging, ideas. Innovation, on the other hand, is the successful implementation of those ideas on a commercial basis. In a brainstorming session, you don't criticize ideas before they're fully formed. That would be counter-productive. Evaluation comes in at the innovation stage, where you're turning good ideas into a commercial proposition. It follows that you cannot be both creative and innovative at the same time.

For making a discovery is one thing; exploiting it quite another, as the Xerox Research Centre found out to its cost when its system for making personal computers easier to use was copied by Apple Macintosh. Apple led the market for almost ten years with the enormously successful desktop system it 'borrowed' from Xerox. But Apple had the foresight to copyright the system. Xerox didn't. Originality, it seems, is the art of concealing your source, and too many companies fail to see an opportunity until it ceases to be one.

Summary

1. The first two paragraphs of the article you have just read were actually a true story. Without looking back at the text, exchange stories with someone who read the other article. What do you think is the moral of their story?

2. Work with a partner who read the same article as you to produce a 60-word summary of the rest of the text. You need only mention the important points, but you must use **exactly** 60 words.

3. Read your summary out to someone who read the other article. Answer any questions they may have.

4. Quickly read through the other article to see if the summary you were given is accurate.

Find the Expressions

Look back at the article *Bright Ideas*. Find the words and expressions which mean:

1. is frustrated
2. has gone wrong
3. a master plan
4. unexpected opportunities
5. failed badly
6. is obvious

Look back at the article *The Lateral Thinker*. Find the words and expressions which mean:

7. a creative environment
8. it's not by chance that
9. management expert
10. idea-generating meeting
11. viable enterprise
12. not telling people where you got the idea

From the articles list:

13. three words you want to use more often.
14. three word partnerships you need, with their equivalents in your own language.
15. three longer expressions with their equivalents in your own language.

LANGUAGE FOCUS

Word Partnerships 1

Complete the presentation extract below by matching the two halves of each sentence. Referring back to the articles may help you.

1. As you know, in our view, too many companies fail to see . . .
2. So what we try to do is to create . . .
3. Indeed, we see such creative strategies . . .
4. Nevertheless, you don't need me to tell you that the launch of our latest product . . .
5. And, no doubt, you'd like to know why we haven't been able to turn what looked like a great idea . . .
6. Well, the main difficulties we've had . . .
7. And the key to . . .
8. You see, this new product is extremely advanced, and, clearly, we should have taken . . .
9. The ideal solution would have been to simply add new features to our old system, and it's . . .
10. With hindsight, we know what we did wrong, but, as always, the secret is . . .

a. . . . to think of these things in the first place.
b. . . . the whole problem really is technology.
c. . . . a climate for creativity in everything that we do.
d. . . . advantage of existing technology instead of redesigning the whole system from scratch.
e. . . . into a commercial proposition.
f. . . . an opportunity until it ceases to be one.
g. . . . to face have been technical.
h. . . . as vital to our survival.
i. . . . a pity this didn't occur to us sooner.
j. . . . has backfired badly.

1		2		3		4		5		6		7		8		9		10	

Presenting

Read the extract aloud, as if you were giving a presentation. Read it two, three, or more times, until you feel it sounds clear, positive and effective.

Discuss

What impact has your company made on the market it operates in? Has it made any breakthroughs in its field?
Has the launch of any of your company's new products or services ever backfired?

When do you say......

1. Believe me, we've really done our homework on this one.
2. Look, let's not make a mountain out of a molehill.
3. Well, we'll just have to make the best of a bad job.
4. Well, we'll just have to make do, won't we?

Word Partnerships 2

Group the following verbs according to whether they form strong word partnerships with *research*, *problems* or *ideas*. Some of them belong to more than one group.

solve	fund	implement
carry out	generate	create
put money into	face	develop
brainstorm	tackle	promote
define	come up with	have
come up against	cut back on	cause

	research
	problems
	ideas

68

Word Partnerships 3

Now complete the following using some of the verbs from the previous exercise:

Companies who are prepared to (1) . . . . research know that it will be money well spent. Many research-driven companies will even go so far as to invest up to 20% of their turnover in new research in the hope that their R&D team can (2) . . . . at least one new idea which will ensure the company's future profitability. And companies who, in times of recession, decide to (3) . . . . research are probably making a big mistake.

These days it is the business of all departments within a company to (4) . . . . as many ideas on improving the business as possible, some of which, if (5) . . . . further may turn out to be major breakthroughs, for the R&D department is not always in the best position to (6) . . . . a particular problem, let alone (7) . . . . it. Of course, you may have to toy with an idea for quite some time before you can see a way to actually (8) . . . . it, and it is this implementation stage which is the test of a really good idea.

Underline all the word partnerships you can find in the paragraph above.

Make and Do

There is a guide to the basic use of these two words in English:
You *do an activity*, but you *make a product*. Look at these two examples:
 Have you done the copying?
 Have you made the copies?
As well as this basic use, both words are used in fixed expressions which you need to learn.

Word Partnerships 4

You can make lots of useful business phrases with the verbs *make* and *do*. But do you know which ones to use? Which of the following words are used with *make* and which with *do*? A few of them can be used with both but the meaning sometimes changes:

business	a decision
research	money
progress	a project
tests	a survey
a breakthrough	a mistake
an impact	a deal
a discovery	a good job
a comment	an offer
an effort	a profit
a loss	a report
a phone-call	a rush-job
a proposal	arrangements
recommendations	an excuse
a presentation	an improvement
an appointment	a comparison
a feasibility study	

MAKE	DO	MAKE / DO

LANGUAGE FOCUS

Word Partnerships 5

Cross out any adverbs which do not fit.

1. New patent registrations declined → sharply/considerably/encouragingly/disappointingly.
2. The old model was phased out → dramatically/gradually/suddenly/eventually.
3. R & D expenditure rose → promisingly/steadily/significantly/tremendously.
4. Eurotunnel shares fluctuated → slightly/wildly/slowly/noticeably.

Eurotunnel was a triumph of engineering innovation. What will be the next great innovative project?

Problem-solving

Put the following stages in the problem-solving process into the most likely chronological order. Are there any alternative orders?

a. Reformulate the problem in different ways.
b. Implement your idea.
c. Break the problem down into parts.
d. Eliminate non-starters.
e. Define the basic problem.
f. Select the best possible solution.
g. Brainstorm possible solutions.

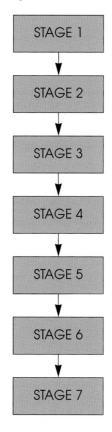

STAGE 1

STAGE 2

STAGE 3

STAGE 4

STAGE 5

STAGE 6

STAGE 7

Discuss

What kind of problems do you have to face on a daily basis at work?
What's the biggest headache in your job? How do you deal with it?

Idea Killers

The following 'idea killers' should sound familiar. They are the kind of objections people always raise when new ideas are presented. The words are mixed up. Can you rearrange them? The first word is in the right place.

1. It cost much would too.

2. It too would take long.

3. Our would that for go customers never.

4. We work that it before tried and didn't.

5. I never boss agree get to the it could to.

6. Now time isn't to the trying be new anything.

7. Don't we've thought already think you that of?

8. It's nice but get never it idea a we could work to.

Discuss

How would you deal with each of these objections? Have you ever 'killed off' someone else's idea and later regretted it or had an idea of your own rejected which you still believe would have worked?
Do you personally like change at work, or in your private life, or do you prefer a steady world, where things go on in the same old way?

LANGUAGE FOCUS

The Function of an Executive

The following description of an executive is meant to be a joke – or is it? Can you work out what the missing words might be?

"As nearly everyone knows, an executive has practically nothing to do except to decide what is to be done; to tell someone to 1. . . . . it; to listen to reasons why it should not be 2. . . . . , why it should be done by 3. . . . . else, or why it should be done in a different 4. . . . . ; to follow up to see if the thing has been done; to discover that it has 5. . . . . ; to enquire why; to listen to feeble 6. . . . . from the person who should have done it; to follow it 7. . . . . again to see if the thing has been done, only to discover that it has now been done, but 8. . . . . ; to point 9. . . . . how it should have been done; to conclude that until it can be redone it may as well be 10. . . . . how it is; to wonder if it is not time to get 11. . . . . of a person who cannot do *anything* right; to reflect that he has a wife and 12. . . . . , and that any successor would probably be just as bad – and maybe 13. . . . . ; to consider how much simpler it would have been and how much better the thing would have been done if one had done it 14. . . . . in the first 15. . . . . ; to reflect sadly that one could have done it right in twenty minutes, and, as things turned 16. . . . . , one has had to spend two days to find out why it has taken three weeks for someone else to do it wrong."

From *The Official High-Flier's Handbook* by Philip Jenks, Jim Fisk & Robert Barron.

Discuss

Is there actually any truth in this? Is delegation just a myth?
Do you agree that "if you want a thing done properly, you've got to do it yourself"?
Who is the worst person you have ever had working for you?

FLUENCY WORK

Brainstorm

"The best way to get good ideas is to have lots of ideas", Linus Pauling, Nobel prizewinner.

Thanks to a computer error, your company's production plant has managed to manufacture 3 million useless plastic cubes by mistake! The 5cm cubes are white in colour, rigid, and hollow. Unfortunately, it would not be economical to reprocess them and they are not recyclable. Minor modifications could be made, however.

Form yourselves into 'thinktanks' of three or four members and give yourselves ten minutes to brainstorm as many possible uses for the cubes as you can. Write them all down. Select the best idea you can come up with and present it to the other groups. Vote for the overall best solution.

Discuss

Do you like brainstorming or do you prefer to work things out alone?

Idea Generators

How about ...?
Couldn't we ...?
Suppose we ...
We could try ...
In what way could we ...?
How could we change ...?
What if we ...?
What would happen if ...?
Wouldn't it be fun if ...?
It's just an idea, but why don't we ...?

Define the problem

Can it be broken down and reformulated?

Brainstorm as many ideas as you can in 10 minutes

Eliminate non-starters

Present your best solution

Sales Techniques

Tough talk or soft soap?

Everybody everywhere every day is selling something. Sometimes it's a product. Sometimes it's a service. Sometimes it's an idea. Sometimes it's just themselves.

Put the following advice on selling into what you consider to be its order of importance.

a. Minimize the customer's chances to say 'no'.
b. Follow up as many leads as possible.
c. Secure as many sales appointments as possible.
d. Listen to the customer.
e. Don't take 'no' for an answer.
f. Keep smiling!
g. Don't waste time on people who aren't going to buy.
h. Don't give the customer too much time to think.
i. Ask questions that force the customer to say 'yes'.
j. Spend time with the customer.

Discuss

How would you describe your own attitude as a buyer: receptive, cautious, sceptical, resistant, hostile?
When was the last time a salesperson tried to sell you something? Did you buy it?
Work in two groups. One group should read *The Soft Sell*. The other should read *The Hard Sell*.

The Soft Sell

"First the bad news. Selling doesn't work. Selling doesn't work because buyers don't like people selling things to them and all your so-called sales tactics just turn buyers off. Let me ask you something. Did you ever learn the hundred best ways to close a sale? And do they work? Of course, they don't. Do you know why? Because it's all garbage, that's why!

"Are you the kind of person who won't take 'no' for an answer? So how come you keep getting 'no' for an answer? Has it ever struck you that you could be doing something wrong? What if you really can't persuade people to do things they don't want to? And did it ever cross your mind that the customer may not actually need your product? Hard to accept, I know, but it's a possibility.

"Now the good news. Forget conventional wisdom. It's not your job to get people to buy but to find out if there's a basis for doing business. Manage the demand that's there. That's all you have to do.

"I know what you're thinking. You're thinking, hell, if I did that, I'd never sell anything. But that's just where you're wrong. If they say 'no', accept 'no'. You're wasting time making contacts with people who aren't ready to buy. You don't need to pitch for business. Stop selling and start listening.

"It was Eric Berne who said: 'Everyone in the world just wants to be listened to, but they seldom get what they want because so does everyone else'. I can see some of you know what I'm talking about. Well, so you should, because some of the worst listeners I know work in sales. Try shutting up for a change.

"Listen to everything the customer says. Give them every opportunity to disqualify themselves as a serious prospect. And since that's all you're trying to establish, it needn't be a blow to your ego to be told 'no'. If they say 'no', don't argue with them. Nobody ever won an argument with a customer.

"Don't make extravagant claims for your product. And listen when the customer asks questions - even silly questions. People ask silly questions for a reason. Remember, the decision to buy is the buyer's responsibility, not yours.

"I know it sounds obvious, but honesty sells. These days people take a little longer to make buying decisions. Let them. Quick deals fall through and buyers prefer to do business with people who are prepared to spend time with them, inform them, and then leave them alone. You see, you can't actually make people buy anything. But if they want to buy, what you can do is make them want to buy from *you*.

"So what it comes down to in the end is trust. Let's face it, it's natural for the customer to be sceptical. Selling always causes customer resistance. It's a fact of life. But if selling causes customer resistance, no selling equals no resistance. And you make more sales when you stop trying to sell."

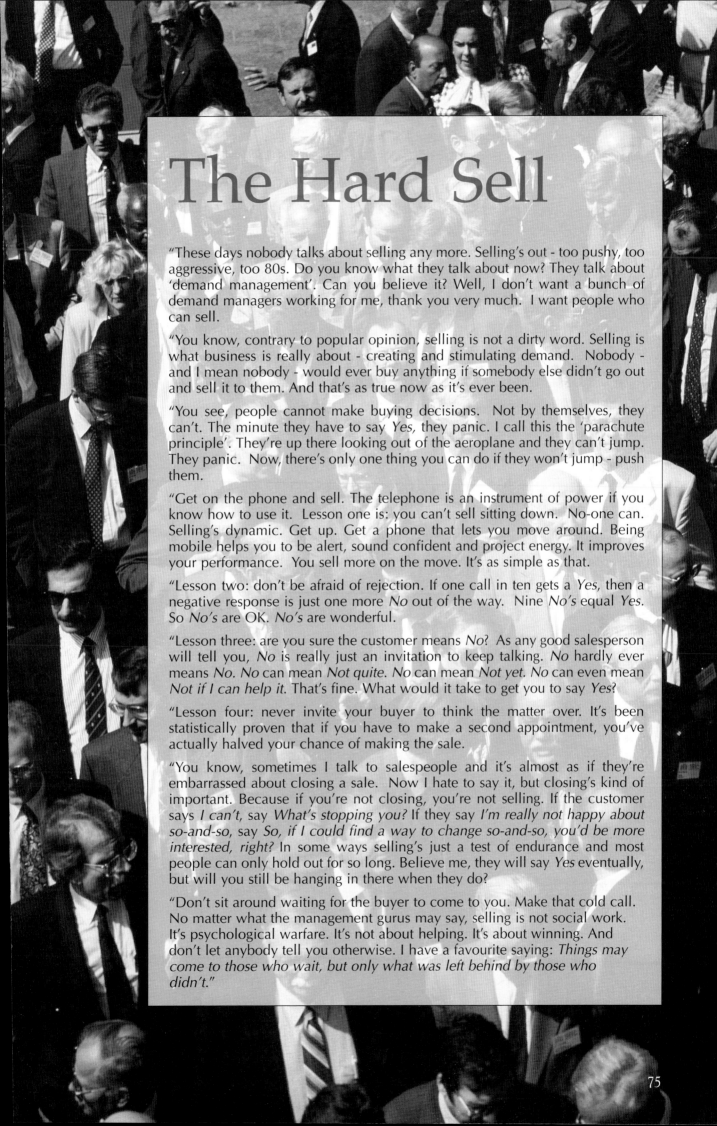

The Hard Sell

"These days nobody talks about selling any more. Selling's out - too pushy, too aggressive, too 80s. Do you know what they talk about now? They talk about 'demand' management'. Can you believe it? Well, I don't want a bunch of demand managers working for me, thank you very much. I want people who can sell.

"You know, contrary to popular opinion, selling is not a dirty word. Selling is what business is really about - creating and stimulating demand. Nobody - and I mean nobody - would ever buy anything if somebody else didn't go out and sell it to them. And that's as true now as it's ever been.

"You see, people cannot make buying decisions. Not by themselves, they can't. The minute they have to say *Yes*, they panic. I call this the 'parachute principle'. They're up there looking out of the aeroplane and they can't jump. They panic. Now, there's only one thing you can do if they won't jump - push them.

"Get on the phone and sell. The telephone is an instrument of power if you know how to use it. Lesson one is: you can't sell sitting down. No-one can. Selling's dynamic. Get up. Get a phone that lets you move around. Being mobile helps you to be alert, sound confident and project energy. It improves your performance. You sell more on the move. It's as simple as that.

"Lesson two: don't be afraid of rejection. If one call in ten gets a *Yes*, then a negative response is just one more *No* out of the way. Nine *No's* equal *Yes*. So *No's* are OK. *No's* are wonderful.

"Lesson three: are you sure the customer means *No*? As any good salesperson will tell you, *No* is really just an invitation to keep talking. *No* hardly ever means *No*. *No* can mean *Not quite*. *No* can mean *Not yet*. *No* can even mean *Not if I can help it*. That's fine. What would it take to get you to say *Yes*?

"Lesson four: never invite your buyer to think the matter over. It's been statistically proven that if you have to make a second appointment, you've actually halved your chance of making the sale.

"You know, sometimes I talk to salespeople and it's almost as if they're embarrassed about closing a sale. Now I hate to say it, but closing's kind of important. Because if you're not closing, you're not selling. If the customer says *I can't*, say *What's stopping you?* If they say *I'm really not happy about so-and-so*, say *So, if I could find a way to change so-and-so, you'd be more interested, right?* In some ways selling's just a test of endurance and most people can only hold out for so long. Believe me, they will say *Yes* eventually, but will you still be hanging in there when they do?

"Don't sit around waiting for the buyer to come to you. Make that cold call. No matter what the management gurus may say, selling is not social work. It's psychological warfare. It's not about helping. It's about winning. And don't let anybody tell you otherwise. I have a favourite saying: *Things may come to those who wait, but only what was left behind by those who didn't.*"

LANGUAGE FOCUS

Recall

Without referring back to the presentation you read, how much can you remember about the following points:

1. Selling
2. Demand
3. Rejection
4. The phone
5. Closing
6. Buying decisions
7. Taking your time

Now exchange information with someone who read the other presentation.

Which is closer to your own view of selling – the hard sell or the soft sell? Compare your views within the group.

Word Partnerships 1

Which of the following words describe the sales trends below?

sluggish   **booming**   **plunging**
static   **brisk**

SALES are

1. . . . . ↗
2. . . . . ↗
3. . . . . →
4. . . . . →
5. . . . . ↘

Word Partnerships 2

All the nouns below form strong word partnerships with the word *sales*. But the vowels are missing from each noun. How many can you work out?

SALES

1. f _ g _ r _ s
2. r _ p r _ s _ n t _ t _ v _
3. t _ c h n _ q _ _
4. v _ l _ m _
5. _ r _ _
6. t _ x

Now complete the following using some of the nouns above and adjectives from Word Partnerships 1:

7. Each . . . . is allocated his or her own . . . . or territory.

8. When . . . . are . . . . you are maintaining your current . . . .

9. Don't worry. I know . . . . are a bit . . . ., but I suppose it could be worse.

Closing the Sale

Match up the customer resistance below with the appropriate salesperson's response:

CUSTOMER RESISTANCE

1. I can't.
2. I'd like to think about it.
3. I never make a decision without consulting my partner.
4. I'm really not happy about the delivery time.
5. I certainly wouldn't want the luxury model.
6. I'm still not sure.
7. There are several questions that would need answering first.

SALESPERSON'S RESPONSE

a. Fire away!
b. I see. So if I could find a way to improve on that, you'd be more interested, wouldn't you?
c. No, I think you're right to choose the economy model.
d. What's stopping you?
e. Of course not. When shall we arrange for the three of us to meet?
f. Of course. Perhaps I can help. What is it you'd like to think about?
g. What about?

LANGUAGE FOCUS

Discuss

"Customers are not interested in buying products. They have needs that have to be satisfied." Do you agree?

How would you describe your own product / service in terms of consumer benefits?

Word Partnerships 3

What 8-letter word will form strong word partnerships with all the preceding adjectives?

final
major
hasty
clear-cut
snap   _ _ _ _ _ _ _ _
last-minute
crucial
unanimous
right

Now complete the sentences below using some of the words above plus the following verbs:

| **make** | **take** | **reach** |
| **reverse** | **reconsider** | **come to** |

1. Even after a seven-hour meeting they were still unable to . . . . a . . . .
    . . . .

2. It was a fairly . . . . Everyone knew what the options were.

3. No . . . . can be . . . . until everyone is present. On such an important issue, it must be . . . .

4. The Managing Director . . . . a lot of . . . . We never know what she's going to decide next.

5. All . . . . are important, but this one is absolutely . . . .

6. I'm afraid your . . . . to close down the plant is unacceptable. We'll give you 10 days to . . . .

7. It was a bit of a . . . . We didn't make up our minds until yesterday, but at least we are sure we have made the . . . .

8. It was an unpopular . . . . , but they refused to . . . . it.

Word Partnerships 4

What 6-letter noun will form strong word partnerships with all these verbs? Some of them appeared in the presentations.

manage
meet
satisfy
create   _ _ _ _ _ _
gauge
boost
stimulate

Now complete the following using some of the word partnerships above:

1. When you . . . . or . . . . , you increase it.

2. When you . . . . or . . . . , you are able to supply all your customers' needs.

3. When you . . . . , you estimate what it is.

4. When you . . . . existing . . . . , there's no need to go out and sell.

Discuss

Think of your local supermarket – what marketing strategies does it use for promoting sales of food and drink items?

*   Buy three, get one free

*   Special promotional price (Until 28 August)

*   Regular Saver Line (an item always cheaper than in other supermarkets)

*   A voucher giving you £1 off your next purchase of the product

*   A free toy with a Three-Pack

*   Oversized packets: 10% extra for the same price

Do the same sort of marketing strategies apply to other industrial products? What about the products your company makes?

Can service industries use similar marketing strategies? If so, how? If not, what are the best strategies for marketing a service?

LANGUAGE FOCUS

Business Grammar

Prepare a set of questions which a client or a customer might ask you about your products or services.

Use the question starters below to help you. When you are ready, work in pairs to ask each other the questions you have prepared.

1. How do / does your . . . . compare with . . . . in terms of . . . . ?

2. What do you see as the main advantages of your . . . . ?

3. How flexible are you on . . . . ?

4. Could we rely on you to . . . . ?

5. How quickly could you . . . . ?

6. What immediate / long-term benefits could we expect . . . . ?

7. What sort of terms can you offer . . . . ?

8. What assurances can you give us that . . . . ?

9. Can you guarantee us . . . . ?

10. Would you be able to . . . . ?

11. If we wanted . . . . , would it be possible to . . . . ?

12. Supposing we said . . . . , would you be in a position to . . . . ?

Quotes

The same word completes all these quotations about business.

1. A . . . . is the most important person in this business, either in person or on the phone.

2. A . . . . is not dependent on us; we are dependent on them.

3. A . . . . is not an interruption of our work. They are the purpose of it.

4. A . . . . makes pay-day possible.

5. Nobody ever won an argument with a . . . .

Do you agree? Can you think of any other words you could put in? Any funny ones?

Discuss

Are you the kind of person who makes snap decisions or do you tend to take your time coming to a final decision about things?

What part does decision-making play in your own work?

Have you ever had to make a major decision which turned out to be too hasty?

Presentations 1

The following fixed expressions were used in the sales presentations. Can you re-arrange them? The first word is in the right place.

1. It's fact life of a .

2. Can believe you it?

3. It's simple as as that .

4. Let me you something ask .

5. I know thinking you're what .

6. But wrong just that's you're where .

7. And as now that's true ever as been it's.

8. And don't otherwise you tell anybody let.

9. I talking see know some can you of I'm about what .

Which of the above expressions are used:

a. to emphasize a point?

b. to involve the audience?

LANGUAGE FOCUS

Presentations 2

Now match the following words and phrases to make complete expressions from the presentations.

THE HARD SELL

1. These days, nobody talks about
2. You know, contrary to popular opinion,
3. Nobody, and I mean nobody, would ever
4. Lesson one is: you can't
5. Lesson two: don't be afraid of
6. Lesson three: are you sure
7. Lesson four: never
8. You know, it's almost as if
9. In some ways,

a. buy anything if somebody else didn't sell it to them.
b. rejection.
c. invite your buyer to think the matter over.
d. selling any more – selling's out.
e. salespeople are embarrassed about closing a sale.
f. sell sitting down – no-one can.
g. selling is just a test of endurance.
h. the customer means No?
i. 'selling' is not a dirty word.

THE SOFT SELL

1. First the bad news:
2. Did it ever cross your mind
3. Has it ever struck you that
4. Now the good news:
5. It sounds obvious, I know, but
6. You see, you can't actually
7. But what you can do is
8. So what it comes down to in the end is
9. Let's face it,

a. forget conventional wisdom. It's not your job to get people to buy.
b. make people buy anything.
c. it's natural for the customer to be sceptical.
d. you could be doing something wrong?
e. make them want to buy from you.
f. that the customer may not actually need your product?
g. trust.
h. selling doesn't work.
i. honesty sells.

Which of the above expressions means:

a. It's gone out of fashion . . .

b. Have you ever realized . . .?

c. Put simply . . .

d. This is the opposite of what most people think . . .

e. Did you ever stop to think . . .?

Discuss

OUR POLICY

Rule 1
The Customer is Always Right!

Rule 2
If the Customer is Ever Wrong,
Re-read Rule 1.

The sign on the left is displayed outside the Connecticut store of American supermarket king and retail sales genius, Stew Leonard.

How far do you go along with the idea that the customer is always right? And what are the implications for market research, customer service and quality management?

Sales Presentations

Work with a partner. Choose a product, service or idea and produce a 5-minute presentation to sell it.

Use one of the product advertisements on this page or one of these ideas:

The best way to invest your money
A way to reduce stress
A way to earn extra money
A way to lose weight
A way to influence people

Own an Ostrich!

Ostrich farming – the fastest growth area in agriculture today. Invest in the animal of the future. For an initial investment of £500, we guarantee you a share in one of our state of the art ostrich farms. A guaranteed 45% annual return! These animals can live and produce for up to an amazing 25 years! An investment that really is a nest egg!

Your Own Personal Breathalyser

Never be caught by the Police again! This neat device fits easily into your car's glove compartment. Simply blow into it for three seconds and watch the crystals turn green (Phew! You're safe!) or red (call a taxi!). Only £15.99. You can't afford not to have one!

Nose and Ear Hair Trimmer

No need to use scissors again for those difficult places to reach. Runs on 2 AA batteries. Clean and hygienic. Can also be used for eyebrows. A bargain at only £11.95.

---

1. Decide if you are going to adopt a hard or soft sell approach.

2. When you are ready, circulate with the rest of the group and try to sell your product to as many people in the group as possible.

3. How many sales did you make? Find out who made the most sales within the time limit. Did your product sell itself?

To help you.......

You may like to complete the sentence starters below as part of your preparation.

The Hard Sell

Start off with a question or remark to establish customer need. The following push the customer towards a positive answer.

Haven't you ever wanted...?
I'm sure you've often considered...
Wouldn't you agree that...?
Wouldn't it be in your best interests to...?
I can't emphasize enough the benefits of...
I strongly recommend you...

> Everyone is a customer. Don't take *No* for an answer!

The Soft Sell

Start off by introducing yourself and your product.

I work for . . . . and I sell . . . .
I wonder if this is something you'd be interested in? Some of the things you might like to consider are . . . . One possibility would be to . . . .
Can I just mention what I see as the main benefits of. . . . . ? I'd like to hear how you feel about. . . . . Is there anything else you'd like to know about . . . . ?

> Listen. But don't waste time on people who aren't interested in buying!

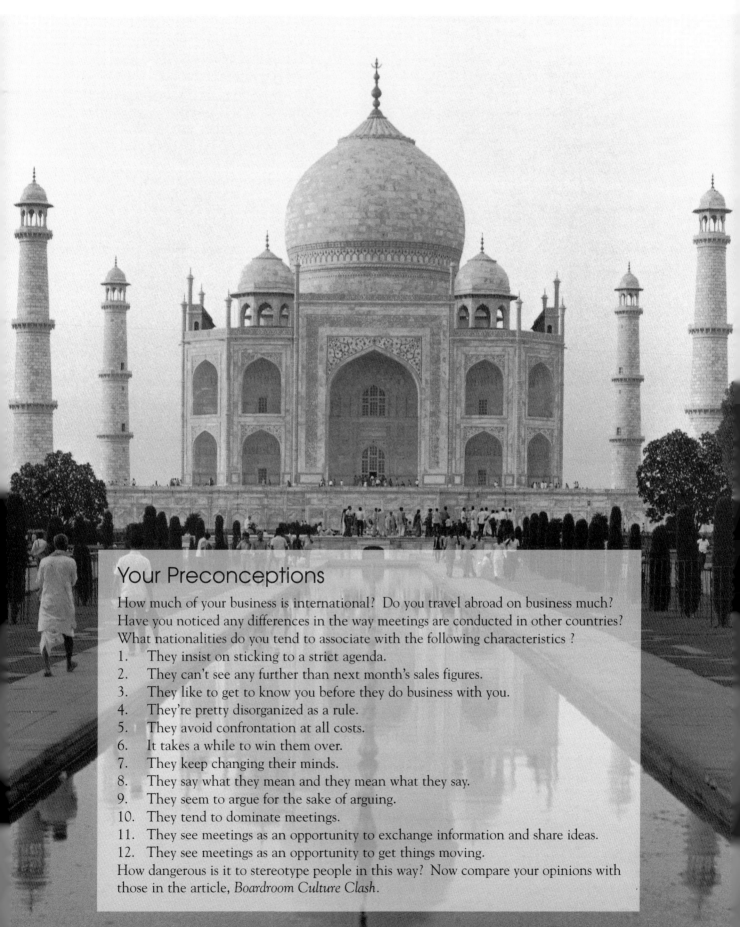

Cultural Awareness

Your Preconceptions

How much of your business is international? Do you travel abroad on business much? Have you noticed any differences in the way meetings are conducted in other countries? What nationalities do you tend to associate with the following characteristics ?

1. They insist on sticking to a strict agenda.
2. They can't see any further than next month's sales figures.
3. They like to get to know you before they do business with you.
4. They're pretty disorganized as a rule.
5. They avoid confrontation at all costs.
6. It takes a while to win them over.
7. They keep changing their minds.
8. They say what they mean and they mean what they say.
9. They seem to argue for the sake of arguing.
10. They tend to dominate meetings.
11. They see meetings as an opportunity to exchange information and share ideas.
12. They see meetings as an opportunity to get things moving.

How dangerous is it to stereotype people in this way? Now compare your opinions with those in the article, *Boardroom Culture Clash*.

Cultural Awareness

Most of us prefer to do business with people we like. And it should come as no surprise that the people we like tend to be like us. So whilst we may dispute the accuracy of cultural stereotypes, it is generally agreed that good business relationships are built on cultural awareness. Across national frontiers 'nice guys' do more business than nasty ones. But what constitutes nice-guy behaviour in a boardroom in Miami is not necessarily what they expect in Madrid.

The US Perspective

For instance, most Americans will insist on the hard sell. It's not enough that you want to buy their products, you must let them sell them to you. They have to report back to superiors who will be as interested in how the deal was struck as the result. Systems and procedures matter to Americans.

The Spaniards Trust you

The Spanish, on the other hand, are unimpressed by the most meticulously prepared meeting and pay much more attention to people. In this they are more like the Arabs or the Japanese. In the Middle and Far East business is built on trust over a long period of time. Spaniards may come to a decision about whether they trust you a little sooner.

Boardroom
Culture Clash

An Unpredictable Affair

Try to put pressure on a Japanese in a negotiation and you will be met with stony silence. Hold an informal fact-finding meeting with a German and you can expect a battery of searching questions. Disagree with the French on even a minor point and they will take great pleasure in engaging in spirited verbal combat. Doing business across culture can be an unpredictable affair.

Animated Italians

Italians too tend to feel that the main purpose of meetings is to assess the mood of those present and reinforce team-spirit. There may well be a lot of animated discussion at a meeting in Italy, but the majority of decisions will be made elsewhere and in secret.

Scandinavians want results

Strangely enough, Scandinavians are rather like Americans. They value efficiency, novelty, systems and technology. They are firmly profit-oriented. They want results yesterday.

Succeed with the Germans

Don't be surprised if the Germans start a meeting with all the difficult questions. They want to be convinced you are as efficient and quality-conscious as they are. They will be cautious about giving you too much business until you have proved yourself. They will demand prompt delivery and expect you to keep your competitive edge in the most price-sensitive market in Europe. Succeed and you will enjoy a long-term business relationship.

Adversarial Meetings

The French will give you their business much more readily. But they will withdraw it just as fast if you fail to come up with the goods. Meetings in France tend to be adversarial. Heated discussion is all part of the game. Germans will be shocked to hear you question their carefully prepared arguments. The Spanish will offer no opinion unless sure of themselves, for fear of losing face. But French executives prefer to meet disagreement head on, and the British tendency to diffuse tension with humour doesn't go down too well.

Prisoners of our culture

Ask yourself whether meetings are opportunities to network or get results. Is it more important to stick to the agenda or generate new ideas? Is the main aim of a meeting to transmit or pool information? It all depends on where in the world you hold your meeting and whether you belong to an individualistic business culture like the French, Germans and Americans or to a collective one like the British, Japanese and Greeks. Indeed, who knows to what extent our views are our own and to what extent culturally conditioned? For in business, as in life, "all human beings are captives of their culture".

Crosschecking

Which of the following points support the opinions expressed in the article?

1. In meetings the French tend to be more aggressive than the Germans.

2. The Arabs have nothing in common with the Japanese.

3. The French generally don't appreciate the British sense of humour.

4. The Spanish are rarely hesitant in cross-cultural meetings.

5. The Americans and Scandinavians value a methodical approach.

6. The Germans want quality at any price.

7. The British tend to be more individualistic in business than the Germans.

8. In business the Italians are more or less like the Spanish.

Response

What are your own views on each of these points?

Well, personally, I think . . .

Well, if you ask me . . .

Well, I reckon . . .

Find the Expressions

Look back at the last three paragraphs in the article. Find the expressions which mean:

1. to compare favourably with your competitors

2. to do as you promised

3. to react strongly to differences of opinion

LANGUAGE FOCUS

Word Partnerships 1

The following business verbs appeared in the article in the order in which they are listed. How many of their word partners can you find in just five minutes?

BUSINESS VERB	WORD PARTNERS
1. hold	
2. disagree on	
3. build	
4. report back to	
5. strike	
6. come to	
7. reinforce	
8. withdraw	
9. question	
10. offer	
11. diffuse	
12. get	
13. generate	
14. transmit	
15. pool	

Choose the eight most useful word partnerships and find an equivalent for them in your own language.

Discuss

How do people generally prefer to conduct meetings in your country?
Use as many of the word partnerships above as you need to talk about exchanging information, opinion giving, voicing disagreement, making decisions, getting results, sticking to agendas, diffusing tension etc.

Word Partnerships 2

Complete the sentences below using words from the following list. Referring back to the article will help you with some of them.

market	price	client	cost
profit	quality	technology	

1. We're a firmly . . . . -oriented company, so the bottom-line for us is not how big our market share is but how much money we're going to make.

2. Even at low prices inferior products won't sell in such a . . . . -conscious market.

3. The market's far too . . . . -sensitive to stand an increase in service charges.

4. We're constantly forced to respond both to changing customer needs and to what our main competitors are doing in a . . . . -driven business such as this.

5. The customer always comes first. We're a very . . . . -centred company.

6. In a . . . . -led business, such as ours, it's vital to plough profits back into R&D.

7. If the price of materials goes up any more, production will no longer be . . . . -effective.

Discuss

Put the following into what your company considers to be their order of importance:

a.   market trends

b.   the price factor

c.   client needs

d.   profit levels

e.   quality control

f.   technological lead

g.   cost control

Is this what you consider to be their order of importance or would you personally rate them differently?

LANGUAGE FOCUS

Business Grammar 1

Obviously, in a delicate negotiation you do not always say exactly what you think! You need to be able to express yourself diplomatically, to make your point firmly but politely.
Match what you think with what you say:

WHAT YOU THINK

1. We are unhappy with this offer.

2. We are dissatisfied.

3. We can't accept it.

4. You said there would be a discount.

5. Don't forget your obligations.

6. We want a guarantee.

7. We won't agree to this.

8. We're shocked you expect us to cover the costs.

9. That's wrong.

10. We want a bigger rebate.

11. We must finalize the deal today.

12. You obviously don't understand.

WHAT YOU SAY

a. Unfortunately, we would be unable to accept that.

b. With respect, that's not quite correct.

c. I'm sure we don't need to remind you of your contractual obligations.

d. We're rather surprised you expect us to cover the costs.

e. We would find this somewhat difficult to agree to.

f. We were rather hoping to finalize the deal today.

g. I'm sorry but we're not very happy with this offer.

h. Actually, we were hoping for a slightly more substantial rebate.

i. I'm afraid you don't seem to understand.

j. We understood there would be a discount.

k. We would need some sort of guarantee.

l. We're not completely satisfied.

Business Grammar 2

Now look at these language points from Business Grammar 1 which help to make your language more diplomatic.

1. What is the purpose of expressions like *unfortunately* and *I'm afraid?*

2. What is the difference between *unhappy* and *not very happy*, *dissatisfied* and *not completely satisfied?* Notice the pattern. How would you change these:

   bad   unprofitable   unpopular   false

3. What is the effect of using *would* in sentences a, e, and k? What is the difference between *that's a problem*, and *that would be a problem?*

   Notice we use *we would be unable to* instead of *we can't . . .*

4. How do words like *quite*, *rather*, *slightly*, and *somewhat* change the effect of what you say? Do you know any other words like these?

5. What is the difference between *You said* and *We understood* in 4-j ?

6. What is the effect of using *seem* in sentence 12-i? Write another sentence using *seem* in a similar way.

Business Grammar 3

Now change the following rather direct remarks into ones which are more diplomatic. The words in brackets will help you.

1. You said the goods were on their way.
    (understood)

    . . . .

2. We're unhappy about it.
    (sorry but / not very)

    . . . .

3. That's a bad idea.
    (might / not very)

    . . . .

4. This is most inconvenient.
    (afraid / might / not very)

    . . . .

5. We can't accept your offer.
    (unfortunately / unable)

    . . . .

6. We want a bigger discount.
    (hoping / slightly)

    . . . .

7. Your products are very expensive.
    (seem / rather)

    . . . .

8. We must reach agreement today.
    (actually / rather hoping)

    . . . .

9. It'll be unmarketable.
    (unfortunately / would / not very)

    . . . .

10. There will be a delay.
    (afraid / might / slight)

    . . . .

11. You must give us more time.
    (actually / appreciate / a little more)

    . . . .

12. You don't understand how important this
    is.   (respect / don't seem / quite how)

    . . . .

13. Don't forget the terms of the contract!
    (sure / don't need / remind)

    . . . .

14. We're getting nowhere!
    (afraid / don't seem / very far)

    . . . .

Discuss

Do you take part in meetings in English with native speakers? Do you find the native speakers tend to dominate or do they make allowances for the fact that some participants are speaking a foreign language?

Is it different when you do business in English when only non-native speakers are present? Which do you prefer?

Humour

Cultural stereotypes are almost invariably wrong, but it is actually quite difficult not to have preconceptions about how different nationalities behave. Maybe that is why ethnic jokes remain so popular, even though they are politically unsound. Complete the following jokes with the nationality of your choice.

1. Why are the . . . . so good at business?
    ▶ When you're boring, you try harder.

2. Why are the . . . . such good losers?
    ▶ They've had more practice than anyone else.

3. How do you know it's a(n) . . . . on the phone?
    ▶ They've reversed the charges.

4. What do you do when a(n) . . . . invites you out to lunch?
    ▶ Fix a doctor's appointment.

5. What do you do when a(n) . . . . gives you their word?
    ▶ Ask for their signature.

If you've chosen the same nationalities as most of your colleagues, perhaps there is some truth in the cultural stereotype after all!

Discuss

How difficult do you find it to express disagreement or dissatisfaction in a meeting in English? And how can you be assertive without sounding aggressive?

Have you ever had a complete misunderstanding when doing business across cultures? Have you ever said something which later you wished you had not said? Have you ever really put your foot in it?

The Cultural Awareness Game

You work for a multinational company which produces computer peripherals: printers, monitors, disk and CD drives etc. But, although these are competitively-priced at the budget end of the market, sales have, in fact, plunged by 20% over the last 18 months. Naturally, you are keen to reverse this trend before the situation becomes critical.

Firstly

Divide into two groups, each representing a different national division of your company. Work with your group to brainstorm as many possible solutions to the problem as you can. Things you might consider include: bigger discounts, price cuts, special offers, extended guarantees, regular upgrades.

Secondly

If you are in Group A, read the notes on this page; if you are in Group B, your notes are on the next page. The notes contain cultural background information about the fictional country your group represents and instructions on how to behave in the meeting with the other group. Make sure you are familiar with these before you meet up with them.

Thirdly

When you are ready, come together with the other group to hold a problem-solving session at which you will discuss your ideas for boosting sales. If you consider it important, draw up an action plan before you wind up the meeting.

Finally

Hold a debriefing session to report back on the result of your meeting and on your observations of the other group. What did you notice about the way they conducted the meeting? How well did you adapt to any obvious cultural differences? Were there any serious communication breakdowns? Were you at any point offended, confused, or amused by the other group's behaviour? How did this affect the outcome of the meeting? How would you approach such a meeting a second time? Are there any general lessons to be learnt about doing business cross-culturally?

Cultural Background Notes

Group A

1. Appoint a leader. The leader's job is to present his or her own ideas at length and to establish to what extent other people's views fit in with the leader's views.

2. In your country business meetings are only held when important decisions have to be taken and it's considered vital to have decided on some kind of action plan before the meeting is closed.

3. Greet people you don't know at a meeting by shaking their hand vigorously.

4. In general, people don't waste a lot of time with 'small talk' at the beginning of meetings, although it is customary to enquire about the family before getting down to business. The family unit is thought to be very important in your country and people who are either unmarried or reluctant to talk about their family are regarded with suspicion. Nobody likes to talk about politics since the political situation in your own country is so unstable, but sport and the weather are considered safe subjects.

5. When addressing people at a meeting, even close colleagues, you are expected to use their family name plus Mr or Ms. In fact, it is quite unacceptable to speak to anyone at a meeting without using this form of address. It is, therefore, essential to establish everyone's family name at the beginning of a meeting and remember to use it at all times. People who forget to use your family name when they speak to you should be politely but firmly reminded of it.

6. In your country ambition and competitiveness are regarded as the prime characteristics of a good manager, and meetings are seen as opportunities to display these qualities. In order to promote yourself you will not hesitate to attack ideas which are different from your own. In fact, failure to do this would be regarded as the sign of a manager who lacks confidence.

7. Although it is expected that all delegates in a meeting will participate energetically, this apparent openness is only surface-deep. In your country companies are hierarchical organizations and, in practice, you will seldom publicly disagree with your leader on a major point. You may, however, disagree with anyone else quite freely and will generally take every opportunity to do so.

8. You have scheduled 30 minutes for the meeting and do not expect it to last longer than that.

Cultural Background Notes

Group B

1. Appoint a leader. The leader's job is to encourage everyone to contribute to the meeting and make sure that they get the chance to express their opinion on every point raised before proceeding.

2. In your country a business meeting is regarded as a valuable opportunity to network and exchange ideas, but important decisions are always made at a later stage and never in the meeting itself.

3. Greet people you don't know at a meeting by nodding to them and smiling.

4. Before a meeting can begin it is customary to spend at least five minutes talking about non-business matters. Failure to observe this custom is regarded as extremely uncivilized. Topics of discussion usually include recent political events, sport perhaps, but especially the weather, which is a source of constant interest to you, since it is so changeable in your country. The family, however, is a taboo subject and is never discussed in public. The normal response to someone rude enough to mention your family is to ignore them completely or change the subject.

5. Meetings are fairly informal affairs and people usually try to get on first name terms with each other as quickly as possible. You would normally introduce yourself by giving your full name but then insist the other person use your first name – 'Hello. I'm John Warner. But please call me John.' Of course, you don't mind addressing people older than yourself more formally if they prefer it, but you would strongly resent having to address your juniors by anything other than their first name.

6. Companies in your country are fairly democratic organizations and people who try to dominate meetings by talking too much generally meet with disapproval. The way to deal with noisy people in meetings is to interrupt them politely, thank them and invite someone else to speak. If this doesn't work, everyone in your group should formally ask them to keep quiet and give someone else a chance.

7. The people in your country are generally quite easy-going and friendly. People who are openly hostile or critical in meetings are usually reminded that negative attitudes get you nowhere. Whenever there is the slightest sign of conflict, you will ask for a two-minute break to give everyone a chance to 'cool down'.

8. You expect the meeting to go on as long as you think necessary.

Quality Control

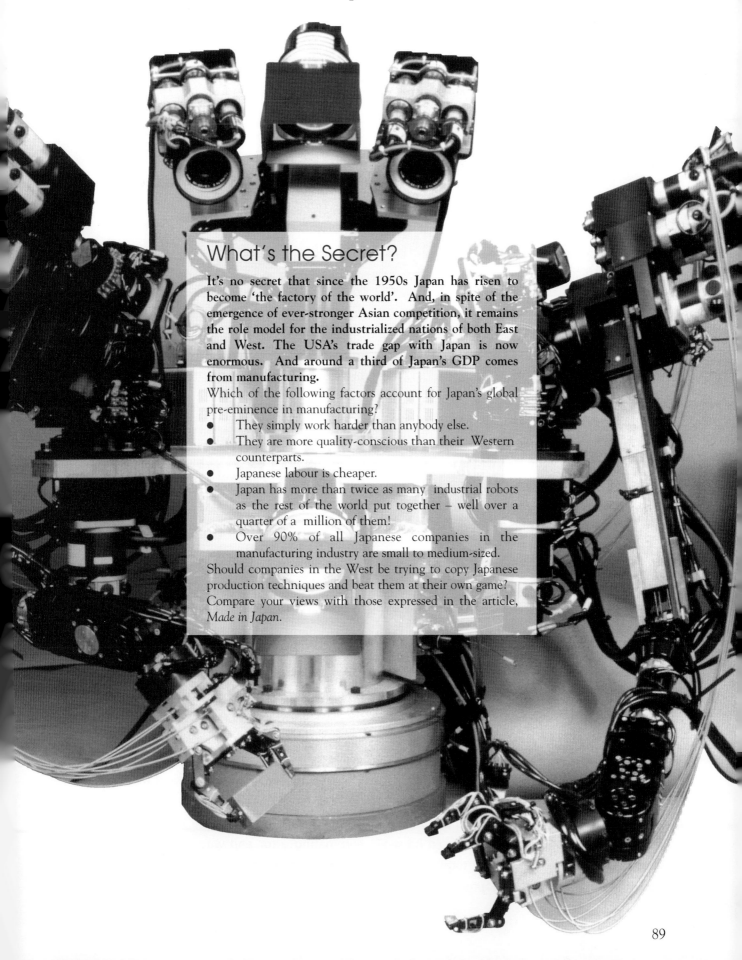

What's the Secret?

It's no secret that since the 1950s Japan has risen to become 'the factory of the world'. And, in spite of the emergence of ever-stronger Asian competition, it remains the role model for the industrialized nations of both East and West. The USA's trade gap with Japan is now enormous. And around a third of Japan's GDP comes from manufacturing.

Which of the following factors account for Japan's global pre-eminence in manufacturing?

- They simply work harder than anybody else.
- They are more quality-conscious than their Western counterparts.
- Japanese labour is cheaper.
- Japan has more than twice as many industrial robots as the rest of the world put together – well over a quarter of a million of them!
- Over 90% of all Japanese companies in the manufacturing industry are small to medium-sized.

Should companies in the West be trying to copy Japanese production techniques and beat them at their own game?

Compare your views with those expressed in the article, *Made in Japan*.

MADE in JAPAN

Quality control is not a new idea. It has been embraced enthusiastically by the Japanese, who learned it from its US originators.

Next time someone gets a little over-enthusiastic about Japanese production methods, just remind them of an American management guru by the name of W. Edwards Deming. For it was Deming who, one evening in 1950, addressed twenty of Japan's top corporate bosses and set them on the road to the manufacturing miracle of the century.

Statistical quality control

It's hard to believe it now, but at that time Japan was a byword for low-quality goods and industrial inefficiency. Deming's advice was simple: successful manufacturing is quality-driven. And statistical quality control, he told his audience, is the most effective method of monitoring and raising standards. If scientific product sampling became an integral part of the production process itself, there would be no need to pay people to produce defective goods and then pay them again to rectify the defects. You would have 'zero defects'. And that is how total quality was born in the USA, but adopted by Japan.

Production management

Ironically, over the last ten years a school of production management theory has grown up, chiefly inspired by and imitative of Japanese models. For from a Western perspective there is much to admire in production methods which the West originally invented but which the Japanese have made their own.

Just in time

One thing western companies have been quick to learn from the Japanese is something called 'Just in Time'. The basic idea of JIT is to match industrial output with market demand so closely that products roll off the production lines and reach the distributors and retail outlets at precisely the rate at which they are purchased by the end-user in one smooth operation.

TQM

Another buzz-word in Europe and the States is Total Quality Management or TQM. It also originated in this Japanese commitment to eliminating error and waste at all stages of the production process. Both JIT and TQM are now firmly established in Western factories. But, oddly enough, they're not working.

Loyalty – the key to success

There's a simple explanation for this. The key to Japan's supremacy in the quality wars is loyalty. Most Japanese executives still expect to work for their company until retirement. And as Japanese production managers rarely have the authority to hire and fire in the same way that their Western counterparts do, re-structuring the team is seldom an option. So naturally the Japanese work together on the basis that they will be doing so for the rest of their working lives. It's all long-term. Product development is obviously important if you intend to be around long enough to see it through to completion. But it wouldn't be so important if you were thinking of making a career move to another firm. Again, it makes sense for the Japanese to be interested in fostering good on-going relationships with their customers, most of whom will also have a life-long commitment to their companies. Perhaps the first rule of quality is continuity.

Commitment to Total Quality

We hear a lot about Japanese Quality Circles - groups of people from different levels in a production department who are assigned to study ways of maintaining and improving quality. But QCs only work if they are open and participative. Too many Westerners seem to be cautious about sharing ideas with colleagues, whom they chiefly see as rivals. That's one reason why 80% of their TQM programmes fail. And, though Japanese corporate structure is changing and lifetime employment may soon become a thing of the past, to the production manager in Osaka total quality is still a way of life. In Ohio it may never be more than a gimmick.

Crosschecking

Which of the following points support those raised in the article?

1. American businesses are now re-learning production techniques which they originally taught the Japanese.

2. 'Just in Time' is about producing goods as fast as possible without defects.

3. Japanese workers have a higher output than their Western counterparts.

4. Total Quality Management means scrapping products which do not come up to the required standard.

5. The quality of Japanese products is a natural result of the Japanese attitude to employment.

6. Competitiveness within a production department badly affects quality control.

Do you agree? Do you have any theories of your own?

Find the Expressions

Find the expressions in the article which mean:
1. helped them on their way
2. was associated with poor products
3. may soon no longer exist

What does it mean?

What do you think the following mean? They all appeared in the article.

1. A management guru?
2. A buzz-word?
3. A gimmick?

Can you give an example of each from your own field at the moment? Are most buzz-words American? If so, why do you think this is so?

LANGUAGE FOCUS

Word Partnerships 1

Work with a partner. Expand on the following points mentioned in the article using the words and word partnerships to help you. See if you can do this without referring back to the text.

1. W. Edwards Deming

guru – 1950 – 20 corporate bosses – manufacturing miracle – century

2. Japan in the 50s

hard to believe – byword – low-quality goods – industrial inefficiency

3. Statistical quality control

most effective method – monitor and raise standards – integral part – production process

4. JIT

match – industrial output – market demand – products – roll off production lines – reach distributors – retail outlets – rate – purchased – end-user – smooth operation

5. TQM

buzz-word – Japanese commitment – eliminate error and waste – all stages – production process – firmly established – Western factories – oddly enough – not working

6. Quality Circles

groups of people – different levels – production department – assigned to study – maintain and improve quality – only work – open and participative – Westerners – cautious – share ideas – 80% TQM programmes fail

Word Grammar

The words in capitals can be used to form another word which will fit in the space. Complete each sentence in this way.

1. PRODUCT
When can we expect to go into . . . . ?

2. PRODUCT
We'll need to raise our . . . . if we're going to match the Japanese.

3. PRODUCT
Nothing was decided and, on the whole, I'd say the meeting was fairly . . . .

4. INDUSTRY
Productivity in Britain in the 70s was badly affected by . . . . disputes.

5. INDUSTRY
The . . . . nations of Europe need to assist those whose economy still depends on tourism and agriculture.

6. INDUSTRY
Sir John Harvey-Jones, the ex-chairman of ICI, and other leading . . . . have constantly criticized the British government's lack of investment in industry.

7. MANUFACTURE
With such fierce competition now coming from Taiwan and Korea, how much longer can Japan continue to dominate the . . . . industry?

8. MANUFACTURE
Defective products should be returned to the . . . .

LANGUAGE FOCUS

Word Partnerships 2

All the verbs below form strong partnerships with the word *product*. The vowels are missing from each verb. How many can you complete?

1. s _ l l
2. d _ v _ l _ p
3. m _ n _ f _ c t _ r _
4. d _ s t r _ b _ t _
5. w _ t h d r _ w   a PRODUCT
6. l _ _ n c h
7. r _ - l _ _ n c h
8. d _ s _ g n
9. m _ d _ f y

Put the word partnerships above into the most likely chronological order.

1. . . . .
2. . . . .
3. . . . .
4. . . . .
5. . . . .
6. . . . .
7. . . . .
8. . . . .
9. . . . .

Are there any alternative sequences?

Presenting

Present all nine stages above in three or four sentences, giving the following details at each stage and using appropriate link and sequence words:

originally   **subsequently**   **then**
however   **unfortunately**

- in collaboration with the Japanese
- over an 18-month period at our research centre in Birmingham
- at our plant in Bristol
- officially at the Zurich trade fair
- throughout Europe
- through the main retail outlets
- last month because of complaints about safety
- certain features
- hopefully within six months

Start your presentation: *The product was originally designed in collaboration with the Japanese and . . .*

Word Partnerships 3

Complete the following presentation extracts using the words below:

mass	line	hold
speed	went	phase
methods	features	halt
step	discontinued	

1. If the unions do decide to take action, it'll obviously . . . . up production.

2. Clearly, some of our older products are no longer competitive; it's time to . . . . them out.

3. I'd just like to highlight what I see as some of the most distinctive . . . . of this new product.

4. The product is customized to meet the client's needs and this makes it unsuitable for . . . . production.

5. If we believed for a minute that the product was unsafe, we'd . . . . production immediately.

6. Naturally, we can learn a lot from Japanese production . . . .

7. But increasingly we're trying to get away from the mechanical, step-by-step production . . . . approach.

8. Introducing more industrial robots would . . . . up production immensely. Indeed, if we don't . . . . up production significantly, we'll be unable to meet our targets.

9. Funnily enough, we still get orders for some of the products we . . . . a long time ago. One of them actually . . . . out of production in 1990.

Look carefully for all the expressions which are used to talk about production.

LANGUAGE FOCUS

Word Partnerships 4

Label the graph below using the following terms:

decline   introduction   maturity   growth   saturation

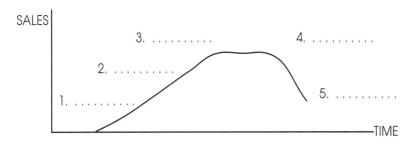

PRODUCT LIFE CYCLE

SALES

3. . . . .   4. . . . .

2. . . . .

1. . . . .   5. . . . .

————————————————————TIME

Complete the following extract from a presentation using the appropriate terms from above together with the following verbs:

launched	**increase**	**stock**	**stabilize**
withdrawn	**exceed**	**phased**	

"Now, the product life cycle describes the changes in a product's level of sales over a specified period of time. Obviously, a new product starts in the 1. . . . . phase. And this is usually characterized by low sales because buyers are still unsure about the product and many distributors may not yet 2. . . . . it.

But once the product's reputation starts to spread it enters the 3. . . . . phase. The product is now much more widely available and sales will correspondingly 4. . . . .

The 5. . . . . phase is reached when rival products enter the market, supply and demand even out and sales 6. . . . .

Unfortunately, the tendency at this point is for yet more rival products to be 7. . . . . , forcing us into the 8. . . . . phase, where supply inevitably begins to 9. . . . . demand.

Eventually, a new product which better satisfies consumer needs will, of course, emerge and our original product will go into the 10. . . . . phase. And it is at this point that our product should ideally be 11. . . . . out or 12. . . . ."

Underline all the word partnerships you can find in the text above.

Presenting

Read the extract aloud, as if you were giving a presentation. Read it two, three or more times, until you feel it sounds clear, positive and effective.

Discuss

If you work in a high-technology industry, the life cycle of new products can be very short. But if you work in the business services sector, you're likely to be more affected by economic conditions and long-term trends. What's your own situation?

Opposites

What is the opposite of:

a. speed up

b. phase out

c. step up

d. go out of production

Discuss

What do you think are the advantages and disadvantages of working with competitors? Has your company entered into joint ventures or formed strategic alliances with other companies to produce particular products or offer particular services? At what level of collaboration?

Expressions with *point*

Can you rearrange the following business expressions? The first word is in the right place.

1. There's point no .

2. Just the to point the get !

3. What's point the ?

4. OK, made point your you've .

5. That's point the not .

6. You point there a have may .

7. That's point the just .

8. I up point to agree you a with .

9. I see point don't the .

10. There's point going it about on no .

11. That's the beside point .

12. I did see point never that of the .

What do they mean?

Match the sentences containing expressions with *point* with the following meanings:

a. It's a waste of time. (there are three)

b. That's irrelevant. (there are two)

c. Don't talk so much. Say what you mean.

d. You could be right.

e. Some of what you say is true.

f. I always thought it was a waste of time.

g. All right, you've said what you wanted to.

h. There's no use complaining now.

Which of the above expressions usually precedes an objection?

With a partner write a short dialogue which contains four of these expressions. Read out your dialogue.

Discuss

What do you think are the advantages and disadvantages of setting up production plants in foreign countries?
Has the company you work for been involved in any major industrial disputes? What were the issues: pay, conditions, productivity . . .?

Word Partnerships 5

The following words all form strong partnerships with the word *point*.

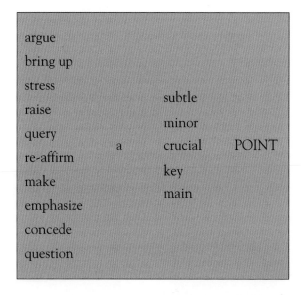

argue
bring up
stress
raise
query
re-affirm
make
emphasize
concede
question

subtle
minor
a   crucial   POINT
key
main

1. Which of the above adjectives mean *small*? Is there a difference between them?

2. Which of the above adjectives mean *important*?

3. What is the difference between to *question* and to *query*?

4. Which verb means the same as to *bring up a point*?

5. Which verb means the same as *to stress a point*?

Discuss

Are you the kind of person who will readily concede a minor point or do you tend to argue every point to the bitter end?
Do you enjoy a good argument?

FLUENCY WORK

Discussion

"Quality is remembered long after price is forgotten", Stanley Marcus, merchandising consultant.

How do you set, monitor and achieve standards in your own job, and how do you go about maintaining and improving the quality of the products or services you offer? How measurable is quality?

Think of a quality problem you are having at the moment or one you used to have. Is / was it a technical, administrative, personnel, cultural or communication problem? How did you / do you plan to deal with it? Complete the first three boxes of the flow chart below and present it to the other members of your group. Answer any queries they may have.

If it is a current problem

Together with your group try to come up with as many possible courses of action as possible. Write them in the boxes. Eliminate the least useful suggestions and decide on a best solution. Comment on how likely your best solution is to succeed.

If it is a past problem

Compare the possible courses of action which occurred to you at the time with any suggestions your group may have. Write them in the boxes. Now report on the action you actually took. How successful was it? With hindsight, would you do things differently?

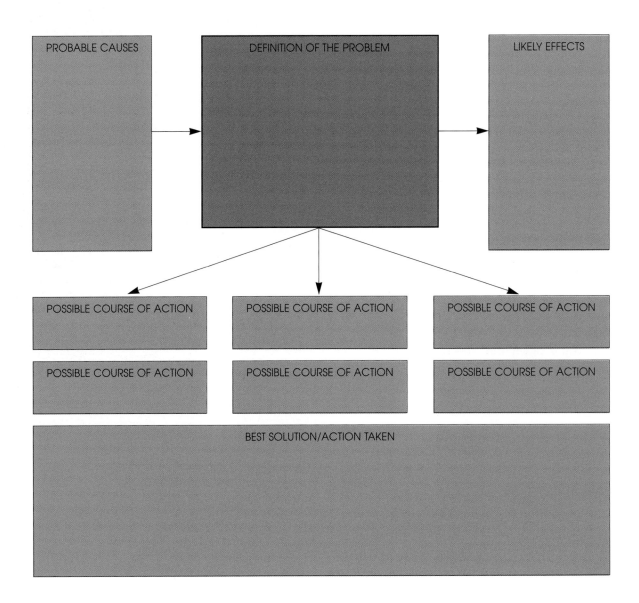

Management Styles

The same or different?

Do men and women bring different qualities to
business or is it nonsense to talk about male and
female management styles?
Mark the following management qualities:

    M, W or M / W

according to whether you think they are more
typical of men, more typical of women or shared
by both.

1. Being able to take the initiative.

2. Being a good listener.

3. Staying calm under pressure.

4. Being prepared to take risks.

5. Being conscientious and thorough.

6. Having good communication skills.

7. Being energetic and assertive.

8. Getting the best out of people.

9. Being independent and authoritative.

10. Being supportive towards colleagues.

11. Being able to delegate.

12. Motivating by example.

13. Having a co-operative approach.

14. Being single-minded and determined.

15. Being a good time-manager.

Now select what you consider to be the five
most important qualities in any manager and
prioritize them in order of importance.

1. . . . .
2. . . . .
3. . . . .
4. . . . .
5. . . . .

Discuss

Does your choice indicate a male- or female-oriented view of management ability?
Is it a fairly balanced view or rather heavily biased?
Which of these qualities do you think you possess yourself?
How do your views compare with those expressed in the article, *She's the Boss?*

She's the Boss

Business was invented by men and to a certain extent it is still "a boy's game". Less than 20% of the managers in most European companies are women, with fewer still in senior positions.

Yet in Britain one in three new businesses are started up by women and according to John Naisbitt and Patricia Auburdene, authors of 'Megatrends 2000', since 1980 the number of self-employed women has increased twice as fast as the number of self-employed men.

The Glass Ceiling Syndrome
Is it just a case of women whose career progress has been blocked by their male colleagues - the so-called 'glass ceiling syndrome' - being forced to set up their own businesses? Or do women share specific management qualities which somehow serve them better in self-employment? As many as 40% of start-ups fold within their first two years, but the failure rate of those run by women is substantially lower than that. It's hardly surprising, therefore, that though male bosses tend to be reluctant to promote women, male bank managers seem only too happy to finance their businesses.

The Roddick Phenomenon
Anita Roddick, founder of the Body Shop empire, is the perfect example of the female entrepreneur with her company growing from zero to £470 million in its first fifteen years. Perhaps the secret of her success was caution. Rather than push ahead with the purchasing of new shops, Roddick got herself into franchising - the cheapest way to expand a business whilst keeping overheads down.

Caution, forward planning and tight budgeting seem to be more female characteristics than male. They are also the blueprint for success when launching a new company.

More Sensitive

When women join an existing company, it's a different story. Less ruthlessly individualistic in their approach to business, women are more sensitive to the feelings of the group or team in which they work. They are generally more cooperative than competitive, less assertive, less prepared to lead from the front. Though they usually manage their time better than men and may even work harder, they are much less likely than their male counterparts to take risks. And, above all, it is risk-taking that makes corporate high fliers. As one male director put it: "I'm not paid to make the right decisions. I'm just paid to make decisions".

Better Communicators

It's an overgeneralization, of course, but it remains true that men will more readily take the initiative than women. The female style of management leans towards consensus and conciliation. Women seem to be better communicators than men - both more articulate and better listeners. And perhaps it is women's capacity to listen which makes them particularly effective in people-oriented areas of business. In any mixed group of business people the ones doing most of the talking will almost certainly be the men. But perhaps only the women will really be listening.

The New Achievers

And, as companies change from large hierarchical structures to smaller more flexible organizations, the communication skills and supportive approach of women are likely to become more valued. It was predominantly men who profited from 'the materialistic 80s', the age of the achiever. But it will be women who achieve the most in 'the caring 90s' and beyond.

Crosschecking

Which of the following points support the opinions expressed in the article?

1. Women are at least as entrepreneurial as men.
2. Most female managers prefer task-based jobs to people-centred ones.
3. Women tend to be more conscientious than men.
4. Women who do succeed in business have to become even more ruthless than men.
5. Men aren't as financially aware as women.
6. Women are more likely to be the managers of the future than men are.

Find the Expressions

Look back at the article. Find the expressions which mean:

1. It's to be expected.

2. It's not the same thing at all.

3. It's not always the case.

Response

Do you find yourself mostly agreeing or disagreeing with the article? What is your score on this scale:

I totally agree!   10

There's some truth in it.   5

It's utter rubbish!   0

Compare your views with those of your colleagues.

LANGUAGE FOCUS

Word Partnerships 1

Match each of the words in the first column with a word from the second column to make nine word partnerships from the article. There are some alternative partnerships, but there's only one way to match all nine.

1	senior	a.	budgeting
2.	career	b.	structures
3.	forward	c.	taking
4.	tight	d.	progress
5.	risk-	e.	organizations
6.	high	f.	positions
7.	hierarchical	g.	skills
8.	flexible	h.	planning
9.	communication	i.	fliers

Discuss

Is the organization you work for hierarchical or flexible?
Are the high-fliers the individualistic risk-takers or the group-oriented communicators?
How about the people in senior positions?

Discuss

What kind of staff appraisal and development programme does your company have?
Does your company generally prefer to fill posts internally or to bring people in from outside?
Are top people headhunted?

Word Partnerships 3

One of the words in each list below will not form a strong word partnership with the word *staff*. Which one?

Verbs

recruit   train   develop   take on
take off   lay off   dismiss   poach
headhunt

Adjectives

full-time   part-time   half-time
permanent   temporary   extra
administrative

Which of the above verbs mean:

1. to hire . . . .

2. to fire . . . .

Two of the verbs above mean *to hire another company's best people*. Which two?

3. . . . .

Which is the less offensive term?

4. . . . .

Word Partnerships 2

All the words below form strong word partnerships with the word *company*. But the vowels are missing from each word. How many can you work out? Referring back to the article will help you with some of them. Can you add some more words?

1. r _ n
2. l _ _ n c h
3. s _ t _ _ p
4. f _ r m
5. j _ _ n   a
6. l _ _ v _
7. s _ l l _ _ f f
8. w _ n d _ _ p
9. f l _ _ t

10. h _ l d _ n g
11. p _ r _ n t   COMPANY
12. s _ b s _ d _ _ r y

Which of the above verbs mean:

13. to start up a company   14. to close down a company

15. Which of the two adjectives mean the same thing? What is the connection with the third?

LANGUAGE FOCUS

Word Grammar 1

The adjectives listed below describe some of the positive qualities of good managers. Change each adjective into its opposite by adding *un-*, *in-*, *im-*, *ir-* or *dis-*:

co-operative	decisive
responsible	competitive
sincere	practical
communicative	sensitive
supportive	assertive
articulate	discreet
skilled	intelligent
patient	loyal
creative	reliable
consistent	rational
committed	approachable
honest	

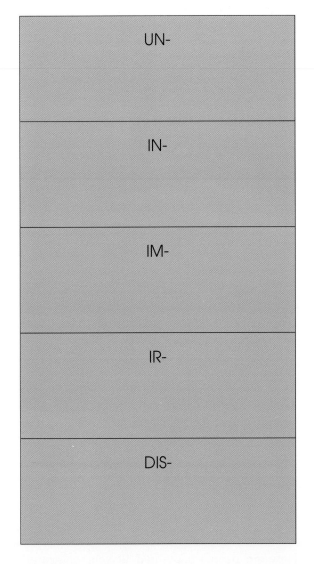

UN-

IN-

IM-

IR-

DIS-

Are there any patterns to help you decide which prefix to use? Which adjectives do not follow the main patterns?

Word Grammar 2

Find at least one adjective from the list opposite to describe the following managers:

1. She always means what she says.

   She's totally . . . .

2. He always says what he thinks.

   He's very . . . .

3. She's very good at expressing herself.

   She's extremely . . . .

4. You can depend on him.

   He's very . . . .

5. Her door is always open if you've got a problem.

   She's very . . . .

6. His job comes first.

   He's totally . . . .

7. She is quick to help colleagues and subordinates.

   She's extremely . . . .

8. He doesn't go around gossiping behind people's backs.

   He's very . . . .

9. She doesn't let her emotions interfere with her work.

   She's very . . . .

10. He always works to the same high standard.

    He's extremely . . . .

Discuss

What's the ratio of male to female employees in your company? Is it different at management level? Is your boss male or female?
Do you generally prefer to work for a man or a woman, or does it not make any difference?

101

LANGUAGE FOCUS

Business Grammar

Complete the following dialogue by adding the missing prepositions:

over	between	out	from
round	with	of	to
in	about	for	up	on

▶ David?

▶ Yeah?

▶ I wonder if I could have a word 1. . . . . . . you 2. . . . . . . that job in R&D?

▶ Er, sure. What's 3. . . . . . . your mind?

▶ Well, you know that Deborah Norman's applied 4. . . . . . . it, I suppose?

▶ Naturally. I interviewed her. In fact, she and Robert Fry both came 5. . . . . . . extremely well, I thought. To tell you the truth, we're going to find it pretty difficult to choose 6. . . . . . . them.

▶ That's what I thought. Only I think I should warn you 7. . . . . . . Deborah.

▶ Oh, really?

▶ Yeah. I mean I don't want to interfere 8. . . . . . . your selection procedure, or anything. It's 9. . . . . . . to you to make 10. . . . . . . your own mind 11. . . . . . . the sort of person you want for the post.

▶ John, will you just get 12. . . . . . . the point? What's Deborah been 13. . . . . . . to?

▶ Oh, it's nothing like that.

▶ Because I know she's got a reputation 14. . . . . . . being a bit over-assertive at times.

▶ Yeah, but it's not that that I object 15. . . . . . . so much. I reckon she believes 16. . . . . . . what she's doing – even if nobody else does. No, it's just that I know you want to make our internal training more cost-effective and I really don't think you can rely 17. . . . . . . someone like Deborah Norman to carry 18. . . . . . . your programme of economy measures, that's all.

▶ I see. And what makes you think that, John?

▶ Well, for one thing, she's always insisting 19. . . . . . . bringing 20. . . . . . . outsiders to run most of the seminars. You know how expensive that can be. And for another, she's all 21. . . . . . . setting 22. . . . . . . some sort of joint venture with MP Associates – more outsiders! I've been opposed 23. . . . . . . this all along, as you know. And so has Robert. He's quite capable 24. . . . . . . running things himself.

▶ Ah hah. That's what this is all 25. . . . . . . , is it? You don't like the idea 26. . . . . . . Deborah taking control away 27. . . . . . . you and Robert. Well, I'm glad we had this little chat, John. I'll certainly bear it all 28. . . . . . . mind when we make our final decision 29. . . . . . . who gets the post.

▶ Thanks, David. I knew you'd come 30. . . . . . to our way of thinking on this. I mean Deborah's very talented. I'd be the first to admit it. And I'd hate to think anything I'd said had spoilt things 31. . . . . . . her.

▶ Oh, don't worry John. It hasn't. You can bet 32. . . . . . . that.

Underline any fixed expressions from the dialogue which you think you could use yourself.

Discuss

How are people appointed in your company? Are there clear guidelines on how to come to a decision about who to recruit? How were you yourself recruited?

FLUENCY WORK

Discrimination

In each of the following situations decide if you would give the applicant the job or not. Tick the appropriate boxes. Be prepared to justify your decision in each case.

1. SYSTEMS ANALYST

The applicant is a 36 year old woman returning to work after giving up her previous job to start a family three years ago. She is well qualified for the post and much more experienced than any of the other applicants. She is, however, a little out of touch with the latest developments in the industry you work in and would require some retraining. Most of the other applicants are younger men.

2. MARKETING DIRECTOR

The applicant is a 29 year old woman. On paper she looks impressive and at interview she came across very well indeed. In terms of experience and expertise, she is clearly the best person for the post. There's only one problem: the job is in a country where women do not have equal status with men and where very few women hold management positions at all, let alone senior ones such as this.

3. PRODUCTION MANAGER

The applicant is a 44 year old woman. You have recently interviewed twenty people for a very responsible post within your company and she is one of the two on your final shortlist. The other most promising candidate is a 29 year old man. On balance, you think the man would probably be the better choice but, at present, your company has only appointed three female managers out of a total of thirty two and you are under a lot of pressure from the personnel department to exercise 'positive discrimination' in favour of women.

4. MANAGEMENT TRAINER

The applicant is a 31 year old man. The company you represent runs assertiveness training courses for women in management and at the moment you have an all-female staff. Whilst the applicant has an excellent track record in management training with mixed groups, you have some doubts about his credibility running seminars exclusively for women, some of whom tend to see male managers more as an obstacle than an aid to their progress. You're also concerned about how the rest of the staff will react to him.

Have you ever found yourself in a similar position to one of those above? What did you do?

ACCEPT	REJECT	CALL FOR SECOND INTERVIEW
☐ Reasons:	☐	☐
☐ Reasons:	☐	☐
☐ Reasons:	☐	☐
☐ Reasons:	☐	☐

Follow-up Letter

Choose one of the situations above where you decided to reject the applicant and write a letter to the person concerned explaining your decision. You may find the notes below helpful.

> **Notes**
>
> Dear
>
> re: [details of post here]
>
> Thank / application / this post.
>
> Whilst / impressed / qualifications and experience / and / performance / interview / regret / inform / this occasion / not successful.
>
> As you know / large number / applications / this post / and / standard / applicants / extremely high.
>
> Should not feel / non-selection / due / failings / on your part.
>
> I wish you every success / future career. We / put / details on file / shall consider you / suitable vacancies / may arise / our company.
>
> Yours sincerely

Working from Home

The Attractions of Work

"The brain is an organ that starts working the moment you get up in the morning and does not stop until you get to the office."
Robert Frost, writer.

How do you feel about the work you do?
Are you in the right job? Do you work to live or live to work? Are you so busy making a living that you don't have time to make a life?

Would any of the following motivate you to work harder? Rank them 1 – 10 where 1 is the least important and 10 is the most important.

1. A substantial pay rise

2. A promotion

3. Extra fringe benefits – a company car, a generous expense account, membership of a country club etc

4. More autonomy in the work that you do

5. Longer holidays

6. A shorter working week

7. A more pleasant work environment

8. An incentive scheme

9. Personal recognition

10. A job for life

With the arrival of the information superhighway and video-conferencing, millions of people may soon be able to work almost entirely from home.

Discuss

Instead of having to go to work, how would you feel about your work coming to you? What would be the advantages and disadvantages of having your office in your home?
Compare your views with those expressed in the article, *Telecommuting*.

telecommuting

If you believe what this article says we will all soon be working at home linked to the world via modem and your commuting days will seem like a bad dream.

By the turn of the century 30% of the workforce will be 'telecommuters' - entrepreneurs working from home with a computer connected by modem to head office and in touch via a powerful telecommunications network with colleagues and clients all over the world. That's one of many startling predictions about how companies will operate in the year 2000 made by business consultant Francis Kinsman in his best-selling book *Millennium - Towards Tomorrow's Society*.

According to Kinsman, the social, political and economic environment of the next decade will favour what he calls the 'contingent employee', a self-motivator contracted by a company, probably on a part-time basis, for just so long as the company needs them. The moment such employees cease to be of value their employer will feel free to replace them.

Likewise, telecommuters are likely to be constantly changing employer, lured by more attractive job offers elsewhere but without the need to relocate. Jobs for life will be rare and it will be truer than ever that "if you are not in charge of your career, then no-one is".

If Kinsman is right, the implications for the way we work are profound. A study carried out in 1989 by the International Research Institute for Social Change discovered three broad categories of employee:
- the outer-directed worker or workaholic, who is chiefly motivated by status and financial reward
- the inner-directed worker, whose idea of success has more to do with enriching the mind than the bank balance

● and the sustenance-driven worker, the born-follower who relies on an employer to provide them with work throughout their working lives.

Clearly, sustenance-driven employees are in for a shock. Outer-directed managers as well may have to offset the enhanced status of being self-employed against a sharp decrease in income and fringe benefits. We may even be entering the age of the inner-directed director.

But it's not just managers who will need to adapt. Corporations too will be forced to become leaner, more flexible and more responsive in order to survive. With competition now on a truly global scale and a fast-changing international marketplace, it is the industrial giants like General Motors and IBM who have been worst hit. For the trend is definitely towards smaller more independent companies. And, clearly, this could have far-reaching consequences. Some say it is bound to lead to a greater emphasis on the innovative capabilities of small autonomous teams. But others point to companies like Chrysler, who have abandoned any idea of corporate vision, as examples of how the fear of corporate collapse may actually crush the urge to innovate.

In fact, we have only to look at a survey commissioned by Shell to see that of the top five hundred bluechip companies listed in 1970, the Fortune 500, no less than a third had disappeared by 1983. And it seems that the lifespan of the world's largest enterprises is now frequently half that of the average person in an industrialized society. As the chairman of Virgin Records in France put it, these days "Companies grow old quicker than their managers".

Information Check

Which of the following topics does the article discuss?

1. The telecommunications revolution
2. Job mobility
3. Unemployment
4. Motivation
5. Retraining
6. Managing change

What kind of worker are you? Outer-directed, inner-directed or sustenance-driven?
Is it fair to divide people into self-motivators and born-followers?

Find the Expressions

Look back at the article for the expressions which mean:

1. before the year 2000

2. in control of your working life

3. going to be unpleasantly surprised

Re-read the article slowly and carefully. Look for language that you think will be useful to you when you speak, read or write English. Avoid underlining and checking every new word. Look for words and expressions which you recognize, but you know you do not use yourself. Find:

4. three words you need to use more often

5. three word partnerships which you think you will need; make sure you know the equivalent expression in your own language

6. three longer expressions which express an idea neatly and economically; again, make sure you know the equivalent expression in your own language.

LANGUAGE FOCUS

Interview

In teams spend ten minutes preparing a set of questions about the article to ask opposing teams. Use the question starters below. Then interview each other.

1. In what way ...?

2. How soon can we expect to see ...?

3. According to the article ...?

4. How will ...?

5. What are the main implications of ...?

6. What will be the consequences of ...?

7. What is likely to be the effect on ...?

8. What evidence is there that ...?

Discuss

What are the perks or fringe benefits of your job? What would it take to make you accept a job offer from another company?

Word Partnerships 1

Can you match each of the words in the first column with a word from the second column to make ten strong word partnerships? All the word partnerships appeared in the article.

1.	telecommunications	a.	environment
2.	economic	b.	life
3.	job	c.	network
4.	financial	d.	reward
5.	working	e.	offer
6.	enhanced	f.	company
7.	fringe	g.	society
8.	industrial	h.	benefits
9.	industrialized	i.	status
10.	bluechip	j.	giant

Which of the above means:

11. a large company?

12. a well-known company with a good growth record?

Word Partnerships 2

Complete the sentences below using the following adjectives. Referring back to the article will help you with some of them.

best	wide	clear	long
fast	far	worst	hard

1. In the . . . . -changing world of business, employees will need to be constantly acquiring new skills.

2. Unemployment has risen, with the north of England and Scotland amongst the . . . . -hit areas.

3. The gradual disappearance of jobs for life has obviously had . . . . -reaching consequences.

4. For many years it was our . . . . -selling product, but now it hardly pays to produce it at all.

5. Opening up branches in Eastern Europe will offer us . . . . -ranging possibilities.

6. What we're looking for are not temporary improvements but . . . . -lasting benefits to our company.

7. Some people found our adverts shocking and I suppose it was a fairly . . . . -hitting campaign.

8. Look, it's a pretty . . . . -cut decision. There's no realistic alternative.

Underline the partnerships like *long-lasting benefits*.

Discuss

Is there a high level of job mobility in your country? Do people tend to move from job to job or do they prefer to stick with the same employer throughout their working lives?

Word Partnerships 3

Which one of the nouns below will not form a strong word partnership with the adjective in capitals? Add one or two more word partners of your own for each adjective.

1. ADMINISTRATIVE
post   error   product   procedure

2. COMMERCIAL
labour   enterprise   proposition   development

3. COMPETITIVE
advantage   guarantee   edge   approach

4. CORPORATE
image   structure   vision   company

5. DEPARTMENTAL
meeting   licence   matter   problems

6. ECONOMIC
trends   growth   company   crisis

7. FINANCIAL
price   forecast   reward   security

8. GLOBAL
market   issue   accounting   scale

9. INDUSTRIAL
giant   relations   output   deposit

10. POLITICAL
customer   party   environment   pressure

11. PUBLIC
relations   factor   sector   demand

12. SOCIAL
climate   problems   change   trade

13. TECHNOLOGICAL
lead   advance   loan   breakthrough

Check the words which are new to you with a partner. Then team up with other members of your study group to check the meaning of any words neither of you know.

Discuss

Have you been with your company long enough to notice any changes in its corporate structure or in its attitudes to human resources?

Word Grammar

Change the word in capitals to make another word which will fit in the space.

1. WORK
The . . . . conditions are very good here.

2. WORK
I'm afraid the project is quite . . . .

3. MOTIVATE
Satisfaction is the greatest . . . .

4. MOTIVATE
A higher salary never motivated anybody but low pay will certainly . . . . them.

5. EMPLOY
Job creation schemes actually do very little to help the . . . .

6. EMPLOY
The longer you remain out of work, the more . . . . you become.

What two important rules for word formation are shown by the last example?

Humour

Complete the following jokes:

1.   Do you enjoy your work?
▶ I love my work. I could . . . . at it all day.

2.   How many people work here?
▶ About . . . . of them.

3.   When does my pay rise become effective?
▶ When . . . . do.

What jokes have circulated recently where you work? Are they translatable into English? Are they repeatable!

LANGUAGE FOCUS

Business Grammar 1

Divide the following predictions into four groups:

1. Definite *Yes*   3. Maybe *No*
2. Maybe *Yes*   4. Definite *No*

Some of the expressions appeared in the article.

1. There'll be far fewer jobs for life.

2. The chances are that managers will have to be satisfied with lower salaries.

3. There's not much hope of the industrial giants surviving.

4. There's bound to be a greater emphasis on innovation and autonomy.

5. There may be a need for companies to become leaner, more flexible and more responsive.

6. The trend seems to be towards smaller more independent companies.

7. There's no prospect of a return to the old corporate career structure.

8. There'll have to be a totally different attitude to work.

9. There's likely to be as many as 30% of the workforce working from home.

10. There's no chance of the bluechips continuing to dominate.

11. There's unlikely to be the same need for middle management.

12. There won't be as many jobs in heavy industry.

Now underline the expressions which are used to make the predictions.

Business Grammar 2

Now complete the following forecasts according to how likely you think they are:

1. . . . . full employment in Europe by the year 2000.

2. . . . . a greater need for specialists.

3. . . . . more opportunities for the entrepreneur.

4. . . . . as many people in managerial positions as there are today.

5. . . . . work for executives over 50.

Make some predictions of your own, perhaps relating to your own field and your own job.

6. There's bound to be more . . . .
. . . .

7. The trend seems to be towards fewer . . .
. . . .

8. There's no chance of . . . .
. . . .

9. There'll have to be a complete change in
. . . .

10. There won't be . . . .
. . . .

Discuss

How would your own industry be affected by a change in the nature of work?

Do you foresee a time when you might have to re-think your career or even consider re-training for something else?

FLUENCY WORK

Are you a Workaholic?

So you think you've hit the right balance between work and play? Try the test below and see if you're working too hard or not hard enough! A copy will not be sent to your employer.

In each case choose the response which is closest to your own situation.
a. = 10 points   b. = 7 points   c. = 4 points   d. = 0 points

1. Do you tend to stay on at the office after hours because it's the only time you can get any work done?
a. Who told you it was the only time I get any work done?
b. Yes, I do hang around the office after work but it's usually because I'm too tired to get up.
c. Well, that's what I tell the family, but I'm often to be found taking liquid refreshment elsewhere.
d. Never. I work hard in company time. Why should I work in my free time too?

2. Do you often find yourself having to take work home with you?
a. No, I get home so late that I don't have time to do any work there.
b. Yes, but I bring it back again the following morning untouched.
c. Only if there's a staff appraisal coming up.
d. Absolutely not. My home is a sanctuary at the end of an exhausting day.

3. When did you last take a proper holiday?
a. Holiday? I'll remember what that word means in a minute.
b. I remember it well. It was the year Kennedy was shot.
c. We try to get away for a week or two every year.
d. Well, we've just got back from Tenerife, but that wasn't our proper holiday. For that we usually go to Fiji, Mauritius, or somewhere exotic.

4. Do you ever take an hour off from work to go for a walk in the park?
a. No. The last time I went round the park I was pushed in my pram.
b. No, but I occasionally go for a stroll round the potted plants in reception.
c. Yes, but I can still be reached on my mobile phone.
d. Yes, I'm often to be found sharing my sandwiches with the ducks.

5. When was the last time you read a good book?
a. The only thing I get to read these days is the trade directory.
b. Well, I finally finished 'Adventurous Cost Accounting for the 90s' last night.
c. It depends what you mean by 'good'. I only read bestsellers.
d. Actually, I'm an avid reader.

6. When was the last time you took any real exercise or played any kind of sport?
a. Does kicking the coffee machine count as exercise?
b. Sport for me is a quick game of Super Mario Bros on the PC when no-one's looking.
c. I sometimes walk the last mile into work.
d. The local sports centre wouldn't be the same without me.

7. * How often do you get home before the kids have gone to bed?
a. I'm just trying to remember if I have any kids.
b. Well, I never miss their birthdays.
c. As often as I can.
d. Always. I'm a parent first and a captain of industry second.

8. * How often do you get home before your partner has gone to bed?
a. Hard to tell. We have separate rooms these days.
b. I make a point of being home in time to make us both a hot drink.
c. Getting home's not a problem, but I then fall asleep in front of the TV.
d. Gone to bed? Don't be ridiculous. In our town the fun doesn't start till midnight.

* Single people can skip these questions if they're too busy.

FLUENCY WORK

Looking Ahead

Now put together a short presentation on the direction you think your company or business is likely to go in over the next five to ten years. Include the changes you expect your company to have to make in response to the market, the development of new technology, new legislation, or any other changes you foresee. Think also of how this might affect your career.

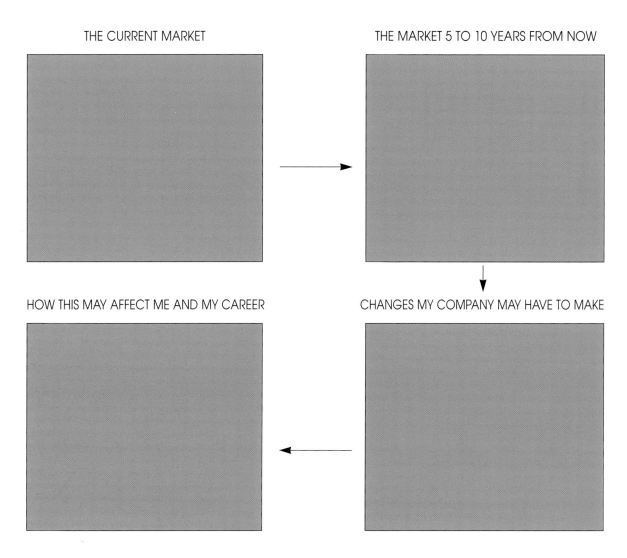

If you are studying with people from different business sectors, compare the outlook for your business with theirs.

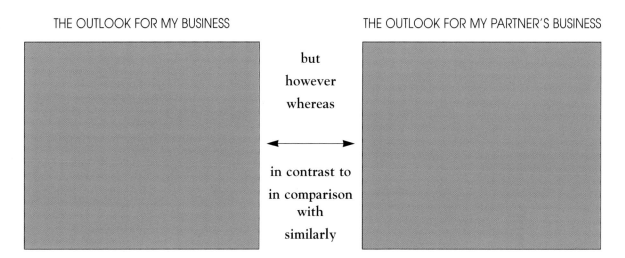

Environmental Ethics

Can Business be Green?

Where do you stand on green issues? And how important, would you say, is the role of business in protecting or destroying the environment? Does the international business community really have a responsibility to sustain the natural resources it commercially exploits? Or is that a matter for the world's politicians to sort out?

The Worst Dangers

What, in your view, are the four major industrially created dangers facing the environment?

- nuclear reactors
- industrial emissions
- the destruction of the rainforest
- industrial waste
- nuclear waste
- carbon monoxide fumes from vehicles
- oil spills at sea
- chemical effluent
- the greenhouse effect
- the consumption of non-renewable energy
- the use of non-biodegradable materials

1. ....
2. ....
3. ....
4. ....

Ecology and Business

To what extent is ecology an economic issue? And to what extent is economics an ecological one? How environmentally sound is your company?

What do you know about the following? See what your colleagues know.

- Chernobyl
- The Union Carbide Company
- The Exxon Valdez

Work in two groups. One group should make a list of the ways in which business inevitably harms the environment. The other should make a list of the measures that might be taken to restore the balance. Compare your lists. Then read the article, *Managing the Planet*.

Managing the Planet

Nowadays, most of us are more or less aware of what we call environmental issues. How many of us conscientiously deposit our empty bottles at the bottle bank, save electricity by switching off lights, or make a big thing of using recycled paper - all in the belief that we are 'doing our bit' for the environment? But what impression are we actually making on the environment by doing so?

Tragically, the answer is almost none. For even if every household in the world recycled practically everything it used, solid waste would be reduced by a mere 2%. In global terms, that would make absolutely no difference whatsoever, because the real problem lies, not with the private individual, but with big business and the $21 trillion world economy.

No solutions yet

Business, just like everything else, depends upon the survival of the eco-system, and you would think it would be in the interests of commerce and industry to learn how to manage Corporation Earth. Yet the fact is that though business is the only mechanism powerful enough to reverse the current global trend towards ecological disaster, it has yet to come up with a practical plan to halt the destruction of the planet.

Poor track record

The track record of the world's companies is poor. Whereas the Chernobyl disaster can perhaps be attributed to lack of funds and the antiquated technology of a crumbling Soviet regime, no such excuse can be offered in the case of Union Carbide. When the full horror of the chemical accident at Bhopal in India became apparent, the company, quite legally, liquidated a large portion of its assets in the form of shareholders' dividends, thereby reducing the company's compensatory liability to its 200,000 victims. And when the Exxon Valdez tanker ran aground, the Exxon company seemed more concerned to reassure the stock markets that its financial strength was undiminished than to console the Alaskans, whose livelihoods were wrecked by the catastrophic oil spill.

Large scale pollution

General Electric has taken what some people call 'corporate crime' to even greater extremes. So much so, that it actually had its contracts suspended by the Pentagon. It stood accused, amongst other things, of bribery and insider trading, and of being one of America's greatest toxic polluters. And one of its nuclear operations in Washington State alone has created sufficient radioactive pollution to charge 50 atom bombs of the kind dropped on Nagasaki during World War Two.

Making conservation profitable

The situation seems hopeless. But, as ecological expert, Paul Hawken, points out, if business is not only about making money, but also about sustaining life, then perhaps it really can make conservation profitable, productive and possible. And some say that, if they wanted to, the commercial powers could actually halt environmental degradation within as little as 20 years. For why must what is good for business always be bad for nature?

Short-term goals

The simple answer to that is that big business is, by definition, antagonistic to nature. Business is designed to break through limits, not respect them. It is about exploring, discovering, mining, extracting, and exploiting. It is quite definitely not about putting things back. Although, in the long term, a living rain forest is more profitable than a dead one, the goals of big business are notoriously short-term. And, contrary to popular belief, big business is not in decline. The largest one thousand companies in the United States still account for over 60% of GNP. With modern telecommunications their global reach is almost complete. And what can the environmentalists do when our planet's greatest enemy turns out to be the only force strong enough to save it?

Crosschecking

Which of the following viewpoints support those expressed in the article?

1. Environmental awareness is greater now than it used to be.
2. People are still largely unaware of the scale of the environmental problem.
3. Domestic recycling is a waste of time.
4. Without government support, the business community can do little to protect the environment.
5. The corporations of the world only step in to put things right after the disasters have already happened.
6. Green politics need not be a hopeless cause.
7. Commercial gain and ecological balance are incompatible.
8. As our business culture changes, the environment will be given a higher priority.

Response

Do you find yourself mostly agreeing or disagreeing with the article? Indicate where you stand:

I totally agree!

There's some truth in it.

It's rubbish!

Compare your views with those of your colleagues.

Find the Expressions

Look back at the article. Find the words and expressions which mean:

1. making our contribution
2. past performance
3. destroy jobs, means of living
4. persuading people to do what you want by illegal payment
5. illegal manipulation of share price
6. opposed, hostile to

LANGUAGE FOCUS

Word Partnerships 1

In his book, *The Ecology of Commerce*, Paul Hawken outlines practical ways in which we might work our way back towards a sustainable economy. Complete the checklist below by selecting from the lists of words:

technology	consumption
resources	hemisphere

Reduce 1. . . . . of energy and natural 2. . . . . in the northern 3. . . . . by 75% . This is not as difficult as it sounds. We already have the 4. . . . . to make things last twice as long with half the resources.

war	inequality
employment	security

Provide secure 5. . . . . for the whole populace. A sustainable economy without job 6. . . . . would only lead to social 7. . . . . and civil 8. . . . .

goods	quality
dynamics	nature

Honour market principles. Since you cannot change the 9. . . . . of the market, you have to operate within it. Taxing morality by charging higher prices for environmentally-friendly 10. . . . . doesn't work. It is basic human 11. . . . . to shop around for the cheapest goods of comparable 12. . . . .

earth	restoration
systems	programme

Extensive 13. . . . . will be needed as it is simply too late to sustain what we have. As part of our overall economic 14. . . . . , we shall need to redesign all industrial, residential and transport 15. . . . . so that everything we use comes from the 16. . . . . and returns to it.

acts	circumstances
society	users

Governments alone cannot create a sustainable 17. . . . . Everything largely depends on the daily 18. . . . . of billions of ordinary people. Humans are not naturally wasteful and predatory, but intelligent 19. . . . . , who adapt to fit in with their 20. . . . . In a sustainable culture people would naturally conserve.

Word Partnerships 2

The following business words appeared in the article in the order in which they are listed. How many of their word partners can you find in just five minutes?

BUSINESS WORD		WORD PARTNERS
1.	environmental	. . . .
2.	solid	. . . .
3.	global	. . . .
4.	private	. . . .
5.	big	. . . .
6.	world	. . . .
7.	eco-	. . . .
8.	global	. . . .
9.	ecological	. . . .
10.	practical	. . . .
11.	track	. . . .
12.	antiquated	. . . .
13.	financial	. . . .
14.	corporate	. . . .
15.	insider	. . . .
16.	commercial	. . . .
17.	environmental	. . . .
18.	global	. . . .

Discuss

What environmental problems does your country face? What are their causes? How do you think they could be resolved?

Does Hawken's blueprint for a better planet strike you as plausible or idealistic? Where would the motivation come from for the business community to change its attitude to ecology and commerce?

LANGUAGE FOCUS

Business Grammar 1

Form project teams. Appoint a project team leader to co-ordinate teamwork and implement decisions.

This project is designed to help you use Attitude Verbs more effectively. Attitude Verbs (*must, may, might, will, would, can, could, shall, should, have to, need, etc*) are essential when you want to express doubt, certainty, degrees of ability and feasibility; they are also useful when you want to give advice or make suggestions.

You have just 10 minutes to solve as many of the language problems as you can. At the end of the project you will be asked to report your findings.

1. In which of the following is spending more money an option?
We mustn't spend any more money on this.
We don't have to spend any more money on this.
Which of the two sentences means almost the same as *We don't need to spend any more money on this?*

2. Which of the following is more likely to be my opinion?
We must cut down on waste.
We have to cut down on waste.
Which of the two sentences above could mean:
They've told us to cut down on waste?

3. In which of the following are you sure I finished the report?
I didn't need to finish the report today.
I needn't have finished the report today.

4. Which of the following is more diplomatic?
That isn't enough.
That wouldn't be enough.

5. What is the opposite of *That can't be right?*
That can be right.
That must be right.

6. What is the opposite of *We should have known what would happen?*
We shouldn't have known what would happen.
We couldn't have known what would happen.

7. Which of the following seems more certain?
We could do it if we tried.
We might be able to do it if we tried.

8. Which of the following seems more certain?
If he calls, tell him I'm out.
If he should call, tell him I'm out.

9. Do either or both of the following refer to future time?
You could ask her but she won't know yet.
You could ask her but she won't help you.

Word Partnerships 3

Choose one noun to form a strong word partnership with all the verbs in each example.

resources	power
the environment	a goal
a promise	pollution
an issue	a policy

1. protect / harm / threaten

2. control / create / cut

3. develop / exploit / tap

4. address / face / settle

5. make / break / keep

6. adopt / implement / abandon

7. set / achieve / reach

8. exercise / wield / seize

LANGUAGE FOCUS

Business Grammar 2

Now match up the rather unnatural sentences on the left with their natural equivalents on the right:

1. It's necessary to take action.
2. It's not necessary to take action.
3. It would be a good idea to take action.
4. It's not possible for us to take action.
5. It's possible we will take action.
6. It would have been a good idea to take action.
7. It wasn't a good idea to take action, but we did.
8. It was possible for us to take action but we didn't.
9. It wasn't necessary to take action, so we didn't.
10. It wasn't necessary to take action but we did.

a. We should take action.
b. We could've taken action.
c. We should've taken action.
d. We must take action.
e. We needn't have taken action.
f. We can't take action.
g. We didn't need to take action.
h. We may take action.
i. We shouldn't've taken action.
j. We don't have to take action.

Have you ever been in the position at work where you should have taken some kind of action but didn't? Or where you needn't have taken the action you did?

Business Grammar 3

Match up the words and phrases below to make 26 common expressions. Some of them have been done for you. Then, with a partner, write out a short dialogue which contains four of these expressions. Read out your dialogue.

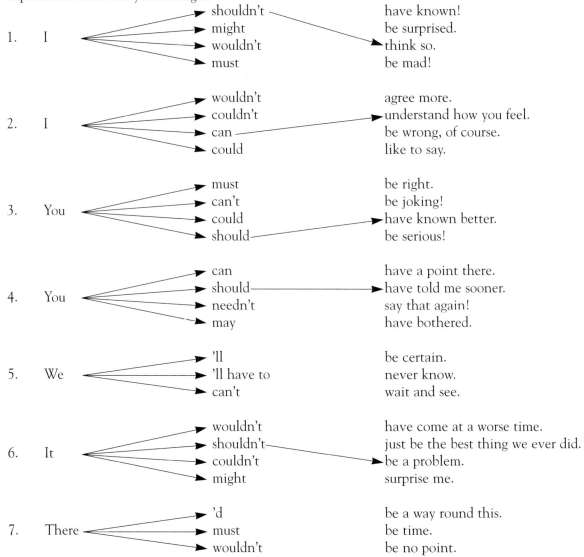

1. I
   - shouldn't — have known!
   - might — be surprised.
   - wouldn't — think so.
   - must — be mad!

2. I
   - wouldn't — agree more.
   - couldn't — understand how you feel.
   - can — be wrong, of course.
   - could — like to say.

3. You
   - must — be right.
   - can't — be joking!
   - could — have known better.
   - should — be serious!

4. You
   - can — have a point there.
   - should — have told me sooner.
   - needn't — say that again!
   - may — have bothered.

5. We
   - 'll — be certain.
   - 'll have to — never know.
   - can't — wait and see.

6. It
   - wouldn't — have come at a worse time.
   - shouldn't — just be the best thing we ever did.
   - couldn't — be a problem.
   - might — surprise me.

7. There
   - 'd — be a way round this.
   - must — be time.
   - wouldn't — be no point.

118

FLUENCY WORK

Business Ethics

Procedure

Work in groups. Each group should look at one of the situations below and decide what they would do. Think about what you would actually do if faced with such a dilemma. Try to reach a consensus before you finalize your decision. Report your decision to the other groups and be prepared to defend it. Then take a class vote on each issue discussed.

The Tobacco Company

You work for a multinational tobacco company. In spite of the restrictions on tobacco advertising throughout Europe and the USA and a strong anti-smoking lobby, your company continues to gross in excess of $30 billion every year. You are, of course, aware of all the arguments against smoking, but you also firmly believe in freedom of choice and realize the huge social and financial benefits the tobacco industry has to offer, particularly in poorer countries.

The World Health Authority is proposing to put a substantial 'green tax' on cigarettes to offset the $60 billion a year tobacco use costs society in terms of medical bills, lost income and reduced productivity. This is bound to affect your sales and may result in widespread layoffs in the Latin American countries where most of your cigarettes are manufactured. You understand, however, that a major political figure in the United States has promised to plead your case with the W.H.O. in return for sponsorship in his forthcoming election campaign.

Decide your course of action.
What reasons lie behind your decision?

The Chemical Company

You work for the chemicals division of an American multinational. A recent explosion at one of your plants in India has resulted in millions of tonnes of toxic gases being released into the atmosphere. Hundreds of local workers employed at the plant were killed in the accident with thousands more suffering from severe chemical burns. But, with such high levels of contamination, the threat to the local community is even more serious. Over the next five to ten years the fatalities could run into tens of thousands.

Obviously, a massive clean-up programme has already been put into effect, but there is still the matter of compensation for the victims and their families to be settled. Although you are well aware of the scale of the tragedy, you also have your shareholders to think of. As your Indian plant was inadequately insured, compensation claims could bite deep into company funds. You might even have to pull out of Asia altogether, which would mean thousands of job losses. Your lawyers inform you that there is a perfectly legal way of liquidating a large part of your assets and significantly reducing your liability.

Decide your course of action.
What reasons lie behind your decision?

The Steel Company

You work for a large steel company in Germany which is currently planning to set up a new processing plant and have been informed that a suitable site in Portugal has become available at very reasonable rates. You are also well aware that local labour costs would be far lower than in Germany, especially as unemployment in the region is extremely high.

Unfortunately, however, the site is one of great scenic beauty and environmental importance. It is the natural habitat of many rare species of wildlife, which would almost certainly be harmed, if not totally destroyed, by the building of your plant. You would, in fact, meet very little opposition if you went ahead with your plans to build, for job creation is much higher on the agenda of the local government than conservation. Times are hard and your firm badly needs to cut costs wherever it can. But company image may be affected by any adverse publicity in the German press.

Decide your course of action.
What reasons lie behind your decision?

The Fast-Food Company

You work for the European Division of one of the world's biggest fast-food chains. In recent months you have found yourself the target of a vicious campaign by environmental groups concerning the amount of waste your company generates. In fact, your environmental record is no worse than that of any of your major competitors, but your international profile makes you easy to attack. Your marketing department is particularly concerned – the vast majority of both your customers and staff are teenagers and young adults, who tend to be the most environmentally aware members of society. Clearly, action must be taken before the protests get out of hand.

One problem is that the polystyrene containers your company packages its meals in may be cheap and insulate the food well, but they take thousands of years to biodegrade. Although recyclable, they are frequently taken away by your customers and discarded elsewhere. The Environmental Defence Fund or EDF, has become so interested in your case that the story looks set to hit the news-stands any day now.

Decide your course of action.
What reasons lie behind your decision?

The Drinks Company

You work for a mineral water company based in France. Chemists working in your research labs have recently discovered minute traces of benzene in samples routinely taken from your bottles. You know benzene has been found to have carcinogenic properties, but frankly the amount of benzene in your mineral water is so minute that it presents no health hazard whatsoever.

Nevertheless, if the story gets out, it could ruin you, especially as you have no idea how the water was contaminated in the first place. You could go public and try to limit the damage to your business or you could keep the whole thing quiet and continue to sell your mineral water until you've sorted out the problem yourself.

Decide your course of action.
What reasons lie behind your decision?

Finance and Credit

Urgent Action

It's an increasingly familiar scenario. You billed a client company for £250,000 three months ago but, although you have sent them one polite, and one less polite, reminder, the money has not yet been paid. Their excuse is that current cashflow difficulties are causing the delay, but the non-payment of such a large sum is now creating serious cashflow problems for you as well. You could, of course, take legal action against your bad debtor, but since they are promising you half a million pounds worth of business next year, you are naturally reluctant to upset them unnecessarily. What can you do? Outline four possible courses of action.

Discuss

Who in your experience are the worst debtors?
The British?
The Germans?
The Italians?
Another nationality?

Small companies?
Huge multinationals?
Government departments?

Who would you give the highest credit rating to? Compare your views with those expressed in the article, *Credit Out of Control.*

Regulation is taboo to the business community, but do we need more control over credit?

They say money makes the world go round. But it isn't money: it's credit. For when the corporations of the world buy, they buy on credit. And if your credit's good, no one asks to see the colour of your money. Indeed, if everyone were to demand immediate payment in cash, the world would literally go bust. But as Trevor Sykes points out in his book, 'Two Centuries of Panic', "there are few faster ways of going broke than by buying goods and then passing them on to customers who cannot pay for them". As if getting orders wasn't tough enough, these days getting paid is even tougher. And with the amount of cross-border trade increasing every year, credit is rapidly going out of control.

Credit
out of control

Companies on brink of collapse

In Germany, Denmark and Sweden, whose governments strictly regulate business-to-business relations, companies pay on time. They have to. Late payers may actually be billed by their creditors for the services of a professional debt collector. But in Britain companies regularly keep you waiting a month past the agreed deadline for your bill to be paid. That's why a Swedish leasing agreement can be drafted on a single page, but a British one is more like a telephone directory. The French and Italians too will sit on invoices almost indefinitely and push creditor companies to the brink of bankruptcy.

Money management the key

But bad debt does not necessarily mean bad business. Ninety years ago the legendary Tokushichi Nomura was racing round the streets of Osaka in a rickshaw to escape angry creditors. They are not angry now, for today Nomura is the biggest securities company in Japan. Nomura knew what all good financial directors know: that what distinguishes the effectively managed commercial operation from the poorly managed one is the way it manages its money. And increasingly a key feature of successful money management is the skill with which a company can stall its creditors and at the same time put pressure on its debtors.

Minimizing the risk

So how can the risk of bad debt be minimized? From the supplier's point of view, pre-payment would be the ideal solution: make the customer pay up front. But it is a confident supplier indeed who would risk damaging customer relations by insisting on money in advance. For the goodwill of your biggest customers – those who by definition owe you the most money – is vital to securing their business in the future. And the prospect of a bigger order next time puts you in a difficult position when payment is late again this time.

Instant access

We might expect modern technological advances to have eased this cashflow situation, but they haven't - quite the reverse. In the past it was common for companies to employ credit controllers who carefully processed letters of credit and bank guarantees. Now you get a telephone call, the computer runs a simple credit check and you deliver straightaway. Buyers have almost instant access to goods ... and to credit.

Be prepared for losses

For more and more companies it's a no-win situation. Charge interest on outstanding debts, and you risk alienating customers with genuine cashflow problems. But cut your losses by selling those debts on to a factoring agency, and it'll be you, not your debtor, who ends up paying the factor's commission. In order to recover what you're owed you'll effectively have to write some of it off. Such is the delicate balance of power between debtor and creditor. For though debtors do, of course, show up in a company's current assets, it is hard cash, not promises to pay, that finances new projects. People forget their promises and creditors have better memories than debtors.

Information Check

Which of the following topics does the article discuss?

1. European attitudes to credit
2. The credit-worthiness of Japanese companies
3. Risk limitation
4. National debt
5. Information technology

Find the Expressions

Look back at the article. Find the expressions which mean:

1. to see evidence that you have the necessary capital

2. you can't get what you want, no matter what you do

3. to accept a modest loss in order to prevent a huge one

Interviews

In pairs spend 10 minutes preparing a set of questions about the article to ask other pairs. Use the 'question starters' below:

1. What would be the result of . . . ?
2. What exactly . . . ?
3. In what way . . . ?
4. What's the main reason why . . . ?
5. According to the article . . . ?
6. What practical measures could be taken to . . . ?
7. How might . . . ?
8. Why is it that . . . ?
9. Why can't . . . ?
10. What do you think is meant by . . .

LANGUAGE FOCUS

Word Partnerships 1

Re-arrange these 'word dominoes' in the right order so that each makes a strong word partnership with the one after it. The first and last 'dominoes' are half-blank. All the word partnerships are taken from the article.

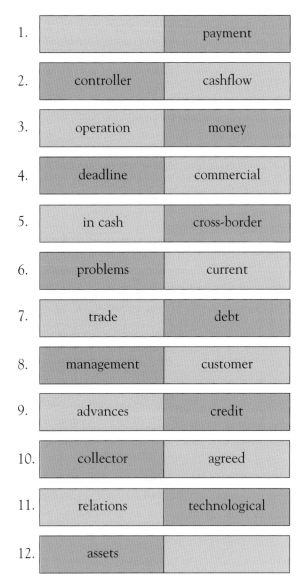

1. | payment
2. controller | cashflow
3. operation | money
4. deadline | commercial
5. in cash | cross-border
6. problems | current
7. trade | debt
8. management | customer
9. advances | credit
10. collector | agreed
11. relations | technological
12. assets |

Going Bankrupt

Have you ever thrown good money after bad on a project that turned out to be a non-starter?
All of the following expressions mean *go bankrupt*, except for one. Which one?

1. go bust
2. go like a bomb
3. go to the wall
4. go down the tubes
5. go under
6. go broke
7. go down the pan

How many companies do you know of where you live which have gone under recently? How much confidence is there amongst the business community in your country at the moment?

Expressions with *money*

Complete the following dialogues using the words below. What do the money expressions mean?

| tight | waste | throw | channelling |
| tied | liquid | bad | made |

1. What do you think of the plan to install an executive gym?
   ► To be honest, I think it's a complete . . . . of money.

2. Why don't we just inject some more cash into the project if it's still underfunded?
   ► Because there's no point throwing good money after . . . .

3. Can't we pay off the loan with the money that's coming in from our subsidiaries in the Gulf?
   ► Well, most of that money's . . . . up, I'm afraid.

4. So why aren't we investing in new plant?
   ► Because I'm afraid money's a bit . . . . at the moment.

5. How much of that money's . . . . ?
   ► Very little. In fact, hardly any of it can be turned into cash for over a year.

6. Look, we can't just . . . . money at the problem.
   ► No, but it wouldn't hurt to spend a bit more on advertising, would it?

7. We've made a pretty good profit for the last three years running.
   ► In that case, shouldn't we be . . . . some of that money into R&D?

8. I don't suppose you could lend me a couple of hundred pounds, could you?
   ► What do you think I am: . . . . of money?

Discuss

Is it really more difficult to work with foreign suppliers and / or customers than it is to deal with people in your own country? How much cross-border trade does your company do?

LANGUAGE FOCUS

Word Partnerships 2

Now match the following words and phrases to make complete expressions from the article. You will generally find it easier if you match columns 2 and 3 first. The first one has been done for you as an example.

1.	to demand	business-to-business	on debtors
2.	to regulate	pressure	payment
3.	to put	immediate	relations
4.	to minimize	customer	in advance
5.	to damage	money	relations
6.	to insist on	the risk	of bad debt
7.	to ease	a credit	situation
8.	to process	letters	check
9.	to run	the cashflow	of credit
10.	to charge	new	customers
11.	to risk	interest	projects
12.	to finance	alienating	on outstanding debts

Word Partnerships 3

All the words below form strong partnerships with the word *order*. But the vowels are missing from each word. How many can you work out?

1.   w _ n
2.   l _ s _
3.   h _ n d l _
4.   p r _ c _ s s   10.   n _ w
5.   r _ c _ _ v _   a(n)   11.   _ _ l k   ORDER
6.   p l _ c _   12.   _ m _ r g _ n c y
7.   c _ n c _ l   13.   r _ p _ _ t
8.   p h _ n _ or f _ x t h r _ _ g h   14.   r _ g _ l _ r
9.   d _ s p _ t c h

Use these words to complete the following:

15.   Well, we were expecting you to . . . . your order last month, but, since we only . . . . it yesterday, it will now need to be . . . . before we can . . . . it.

16.   Although we managed to . . . . another new order from Holland three weeks ago, we've . . . . this one rather badly, and if they end up . . . . it and going back to their previous supplier, I'm worried that we may just . . . . all our Dutch orders before very long.

LANGUAGE FOCUS

Business Grammar

Complete the following summary of the article by writing in the correct prepositions:

by   on   in   up   off   behind

Referring back to the text of the article will help you with some of them.

Most people pay their domestic bills 1. . . . . . . cash or 2. . . . . . cheque. This is often unrealistic in business. But allowing customers to buy large amounts of stock 3. . . . . . . credit is not without its problems. It is extremely difficult to ask a valued customer for payment 4. . . . . . . advance because it may look as if you don't trust them. You can't really charge them interest 5. . . . . . . the outstanding sum either, even if they miss the agreed deadline for settlement, or they might get upset and withdraw their business altogether.

To make matters worse, many companies these days will deliberately sit 6. . . . . . . your invoice and wait to see how long it is before you actually put pressure 7. . . . . . . them to pay 8. . . . . Of course, you can ease both your cashflow situation and theirs by offering them the facility to pay 9. . . . . . . what they owe you 10. . . . . . . regular instalments. But that doesn't mean to say they won't fall 11. . . . . . . with their repayments whenever they're short of cash. And you may end up writing 12. . . . . . . half the debt altogether.

Things would probably be a lot simpler if everyone paid 13. . . . . . . front for the goods they bought and in theory a customer should be able to pay straightaway 14. . . . . . . direct bank transfer. This, of course, would mean customers remained 15. . . . . . . constant credit with their suppliers, but it would also prevent them from playing the waiting game with their creditors and that would never do. Since most companies cannot pay you your money till they get theirs, they will continue to conserve cash until the very last minute.

Underline all the word partnerships you can find in the summary above.

Humour

In Britain accountants are traditionally the target of a lot of jokes, but with the fees most of them charge they usually have the last laugh. Match up the halves of the following jokes:

1. How can you tell if accountants are lying?

2. What do you have if you have five accountants up to their necks in sand?

3. Why don't auditors become accountants?

4. What do you call a former accountant?

5. How do you get an accountant down from a tree?

a. Waiter!

b. Cut the rope.

c. They can't take the excitement.

d. Not enough sand.

e. Their lips are moving.

Discuss

It was recently reported in the British press that a private individual earning just £12,000 a year had applied for and been given so many credit cards he had a combined credit limit of one and a half million pounds! By the time they caught up with him he was already £120,000 in debt.

How many credit cards do you have? How many do you actually use? Have you ever exceeded your limit? What would you do if they took away your plastic cards?

W. A. S.

—

How / when ?

BALAST

wash

FLUENCY WORK

Getting Tough

Thanks to slow payers and a lot of bad debt recently, your company, Halliday Electronics, is experiencing serious cashflow difficulties and cannot meet several payments of its own. The situation has become so serious that you are now forced to get tough with at least one of your debtors, even if it means losing their business in the future. The question is: who is it going to be? Who can't pay and who won't pay?

Listed below are the four companies who owe you the most money. An immediate settlement by any one of them of their outstanding debt would be enough to solve your current problems.

Work in small groups. You must reach a consensus before you make a final decision.

Present and justify your decision to the other groups.

Pineapple Computers owe you £275,000 and are four months late in settling their bill. You have been doing business with Pineapple for over 15 years. They were, in fact, your first major client and are currently your second biggest customer. You know the owner of the company socially and wonder how long he can continue to compete in a market dominated by the big multinationals. Pineapple probably have the funds to pay you if you press them, but it may seriously damage their business. On the other hand, what will happen to your money if they go bust?

Bonnetti Processors are six months late with the £190,000 they owe you. Bonnetti is a relatively new customer and it has taken nearly eighteen months of ongoing negotiations to win their business. Financially, Bonnetti is in extremely good shape with its share price more than doubling in the last two years. You believe that late payment is simply regarded as a money-saving policy in their finance department. And apparently they used to enjoy a fairly flexible arrangement with their previous suppliers from whom you won their business.

Schaudi-Meyer is by far your biggest client, accounting last year for 1.9 million pounds worth of business. At the moment they owe you £285,000 and are two months behind with the payment. They have contacted you about this and explained that it is the result of the temporary cashflow difficulties caused by their recent expansion and, therefore, nothing to worry about. They would like to treble their credit limit and are promising you considerably more business in the future if you can be patient with them now. You feel quite confident that SM will keep their word but you see no way of offering them the huge amount of credit they're asking for.

Jensen & Jensen are six weeks late paying you the £210,000 they owe. Normally this would not worry you unduly, but, since this is the first time they haven't paid on time in 11 years, you are a bit concerned. When you phoned them about the problem three days ago they were unable to offer a satisfactory explanation but promised to get back to you. So far you've heard nothing. A business contact in Scandinavia has told you the company is rumoured to be on the verge of bankruptcy and that you are unlikely to get your money even if you call the debt in. However, there was a similar scare four years ago, which the company survived.

FLUENCY WORK

Follow-up Letter

Write a polite but forceful letter to the company you have selected, explaining the situation, setting out your demands and detailing the course of action you will take if those demands are not met. These notes may help you:

Notes:

I / again / writing / you / regard / outstanding sum of £... / owed by your company / goods / supplied / Halliday Electronics. As I / written / you / this matter / two previous occasions / you must / aware / account / now ... months in arrears   / and so far / received no payment whatsoever.

Perhaps / inform us / reason / this delay. If / merely the result / administrative error / we / appreciate / prompt resolution / whatever problems / you may be having.

We sincerely hope / your company / not experiencing / difficulties / more serious nature / and whilst we / always / enjoyed / excellent relationship with ... / afraid / we must now insist / immediate settlement. Otherwise / no alternative / refer the matter / legal department.

I trust / you / give this matter / urgent attention.

Follow-up Phone Call

As the Financial Director of the company concerned, prepare your case and phone up your creditor to discuss the implications of the letter you have received from them. You may find some of the following language useful:

Let me first of all apologize for . . .
Let me assure you . . .
You have my word that . . .
Obviously, we wouldn't want to . . .
Please understand my position . . .

Discuss

Have you ever refused a customer credit? Would you? How does your company deal with slow payers?

What you'd like to say:

Look. . . . . . . !

This is the third time I've had to write to you about the enormous sum of money you owe us. You know full well that you were supposed to pay up ages ago but so far you haven't sent us a penny.
What the hell is going on? If this is down to some administrative cock-up, then get it sorted out immediately.
Hopefully you're not about to go bust. You've always managed to pay on time in the past, so pay up now or we'll sue.

See to it!

Yours angrily, . . .

Financial Director

UNIT SIXTEEN

Economic Issues

An Uncertain Future

We live in uncertain times, both politically and economically. In your view, what are the greatest threats to the world economy?

- political instability
- mass unemployment
- massive trade deficits
- poverty in the Third World
- the North-South divide
- the collapse of communism
- a population explosion
- under-employment

- racial tension
- hyperinflation
- cheap labour markets
- the debt crisis
- the East-West divide
- environmental damage
- an ageing population
- trade wars

Write down here what you consider to be the four key global issues from the list above or choose others that you believe to be even more important. What do you think their economic implications might be?

GLOBAL ISSUES	ECONOMIC IMPLICATIONS
1.	. . . .
2.	. . . .
3.	. . . .
4.	. . . .

Mark on the map the countries or geographic areas you think will have the most direct or indirect impact on the global economy over the next five to ten years. North, Central, Latin America? The EU? Central Europe? The former Soviet Union countries? The Middle East? Africa? The Far East? The Pacific Rim?

Can you justify your view?

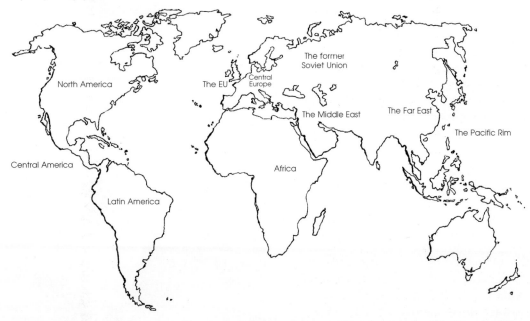

Compare your views with your colleagues and those expressed in the article, *The Death of Economics*.

The Death of Economics

The world economy is falling apart. And no one has a clue what's going wrong - least of all the economists. Whereas, in the past, supply and demand usually had a way of evening themselves out, we now swing from hyperinflation to soaring unemployment as slump follows boom. The once predictable business cycles which drive the market economy have gone completely out of control. The economic statistics issued by governments every month seem more unreliable than ever. And, for the first time, politicians have started talking about 'the death of economics'.

Recession and Collapse
For all its industrial might, the United States can do nothing to close its trade gap with Japan. And yet, in spite of a healthy trade surplus, Japan is itself sliding deeper into recession. In Germany it's the same story. And almost before their economies have had a chance to recover from years of communism, many of the former Soviet bloc countries are on the verge of economic collapse.

The unemployed underclass
But it isn't crippling deficits in the West and post-communist chaos in the East which pose the greatest threat to the world economy. Neither is it the global arms build-up, political instability in the Third World or the Latin American debt crisis. No. The single biggest economic disaster at the end of the 20th century is the emergence throughout the industrialized nations of a vast and permanent underclass of unemployed.

Cheap labour from the East
In the EU, official figures put the number of unemployed at more than five times what it was 20 years ago. In Central and Eastern Europe wages have fallen so far behind escalating inflation that immigration

controls in the West have had to be tightened to prevent an influx of workers from the East. But this hasn't stopped Western companies exploiting cheap labour in Eastern Europe and putting their own employees out of work.

The working poor

In the USA, where unemployment benefit is cut after six months and staying out of work is not an option, they claim to be creating jobs, but only at the cost of falling real incomes. For in many of the inner cities of the USA they have something approaching a Third World economy with millions of people working for far below the minimum wage. In Japan too the problem is not so much unemployment as under-employment, with many of the Japanese, in fact, in low-paid dead-end jobs. If Europe has a growing army of unemployed, Japan and the States now have an army of working poor.

The disadvantaged minority

The consequences of this are far-reaching. It goes without saying that a consumerist society depends on a plentiful supply of consumers. But consumers need to be earning money in order to consume. Eventually, a disadvantaged minority will undermine the whole social system.

The myth of economic growth

Over the past decade it has been popular to talk about economic growth as if it were the answer to all our problems. But, even if there were any evidence that economic growth naturally leads to lower unemployment, which there isn't, the rate of growth amongst the world's richest nations has actually been steadily declining since the 1960s.

Economical with the truth

Current government figures point to an economic recovery. But can we trust government figures? If they say our balance of trade has improved, how do we know that it is true? If you were the government, the pound was fragile and the announcement of a bad trade deficit could cause it to collapse, what would you do? Spend a billion supporting sterling or put out a set of massaged figures? As journalist Richard Northedge puts it, "it's often easier to be economical with the truth than truthful about the economy".

Information Check

Which of the following topics does the article discuss?

1. The boom-bust economy
2. American foreign policy
3. Global recession
4. Political extremism
5. Re-training the unemployed
6. Consumerism
7. The black economy
8. Government cover-ups

Response

What are your personal reactions to the article?

1. What interested me was . . . .
2. What surprised me was . . . .
3. What shocked me was . . . .
4. It annoyed me that . . . .
5. I wasn't aware that . . . .
6. I'm not sure about . . . .

Find the Expressions

Find the words and expressions in the article which mean:

1. no one has any idea
2. industrial strength
3. are on the point of economic collapse
4. severe deficits
5. to be made stricter
6. a mass entry
7. jobs without prospects
8. it's obvious
9. the pound is in a weak position

Read the text again. Find:

10. three words you want to use more often.
11. three word partnerships you need, with their equivalents in your own language.
12. three longer expressions with their equivalents in your own language.

LANGUAGE FOCUS

Word Partnerships 1

Without referring back to the text, complete the following notes on the article.

THE DEATH OF ECONOMICS

1. The world economy is . . . . apart.
2. No one has a . . . . what's going wrong.
3. Supply and demand always used to . . . . themselves out.
4. We now swing from hyperinflation to soaring . . . .
5. Government economic . . . . are more unreliable than ever.

THE WORLD ECONOMY

6. The US is unable to . . . . its trade gap with Japan.
7. Japan and Germany are sliding deeper into . . . .
8. The former Communist countries are on the verge of economic . . . .

UNEMPLOYMENT

9. Unemployment poses the greatest . . . . to the world economy.
10. Western companies are exploiting cheap . . . . in the East.
11. In the USA and Japan people are employed at well below the minimum . . . .
12. The consequences are far- . . . .

ECONOMIC GROWTH

13. Contrary to popular opinion, economic growth is not the . . . .
14. Economic growth amongst the world's richest nations has been . . . . since the 60s.
15. Current government figures point to an economic . . . . , but they can't be trusted.

Discuss

How strong is the economy in your country? Would you say it was about to enter a period of growth or decline?

Word Partnerships 2

Complete these words by adding the vowels. Each word can follow the adjective, *economic*.

1. g r _ w t h
2. _ n d _ c _ t _ r s
3. c r _ s _ s
4. f _ r _ c _ s t
5. f _ r c _ s
6. t h _ _ r y
7. p _ l _ c y
8. _ _ t l _ _ k
9. r _ c _ s s _ _ n
10. m _ _ s _ r _ s
11. d _ v _ l _ p m _ n t
12. r _ _ n
13. r _ f _ r m
14. s t r _ t _ g y
15. r _ c _ v _ r y
16. _ n _ _ n
17. s _ n c t _ _ n s
18. _ _ d

Word Partnerships 3

Now complete the following using some of the word partners above:

1. Economic . . . . , such as the rate of inflation and the level of unemployment, are the signs that economists look for to help them produce their economic . . . .

2. Economic . . . . is what a country faces if it builds up too great a national debt.

3. The prospects for a country's economic future might be called its economic . . . .

4. During a period of economic . . . . the government is forced to take strong economic . . . . to revitalize the economy.

5. Despite all the talk of political and economic . . . . , Europe seems more divided than ever.

LANGUAGE FOCUS

Current Affairs 1

Here are some of the most common expressions you will need when reading or listening to business news. You probably know most of the nouns already, but do you know the verbs that go with them?

Whenever you learn a new expression, try to learn its opposite as well. Choose verbs from the boxes which are the opposite of those on the left.

close	impede	scrap	cut	improve
relax	break off	come out of	harm	privatize

1.	nationalize	INDUSTRY
2.	increase	SOCIAL BENEFITS
3.	go into	RECESSION
4.	damage	INTERNATIONAL RELATIONS
5.	tighten	IMMIGRATION CONTROLS
6.	set up	AN INVESTMENT PROGRAMME
7.	widen	THE TRADE GAP
8.	enter into	NEGOTIATIONS / TALKS
9.	promote	OUR IMAGE ABROAD
10.	bring about	ECONOMIC RECOVERY

help	adopt	put off	divide	push up
neglect	launch	reduce	pay off	resist

11.	raise	TAXATION
12.	unite	PUBLIC OPINION
13.	bring down	UNEMPLOYMENT
14.	hit	THE UNEMPLOYED
15.	give in to	PRESSURE
16.	attract	FOREIGN INVESTORS
17.	come under	AN ATTACK
18.	accumulate	DEBTS
19.	abandon	A POLICY
20.	invest in	EDUCATION

Current Affairs 2

Now complete the following newspaper headlines using words from the previous exercise. The abbreviations marked * are explained below.

1. Britain set to come out of . . . . before rest of Europe, promises Chancellor.

2. Widening . . . . must be closed, says DTI*.

3. Unions furious as Employment Minister cuts . . . . for out-of-work .

4. Montreal relaxes . . . . for French-speakers.

5. Third World investment programme . . . .

6. Europe sinks deeper into . . . .

7. Football hooligans can only harm . . . . , warns Home Secretary.

8. Washington resists . . . . to intervene in North Korea.

9. British Euro-Sceptics will put off . . . . , warn CBI*.

10. MEPs* come under . . . . in Brussels corruption scandal.

11. Socialists prioritize bringing down . . . .

12. . . . . united on Northern Ireland.

* DTI = Department of Trade and Industry
CBI = Confederation of British Industry
MEP = Member of the European Parliament

Abbreviations

Do you know these?
1. AGM   5. NAFTA
2. IMF   6. GATT
3. GNP   7. RPI
4. GDP   8. VAT
What abbreviations do you use regularly at work?

Word Grammar 1

Many prefixes in English have a specific meaning. Match up the following with their meanings:

Prefix		Meaning	
1.	pre-	a.	in favour of
2.	post-	b.	many
3.	pro-	c.	not
4.	anti-	d.	new
5.	non-	e.	before
6.	ex-	f.	against
7.	neo-	g.	former
8.	multi-	h.	after

Which of the prefixes above commonly precede the following words?

1.	European	9.	fascist
2.	industrial	10.	essential
3.	nuclear	11.	media
4.	lateral	12.	payment
5.	wife	13.	specialist
6.	conformist	14.	government
7.	terrorist	15.	national
8.	communist era	16.	war

Word Grammar 2

The words in capitals can be used to form another word which will fit in the space. Complete the sentences in this way.

ECONOMICS

1. She's a leading . . . .
2. You can call it being . . . . with the truth, if you like. I call it lying!
3. We need to think of practical ways in which we can . . . .

POLITICS

4. Politics is too serious a matter to be left to the . . . .
5. The whole thing is . . . . motivated.
6. They've . . . . the issue by involving the government.

Discuss

Do you have strong political views? Is there anything you're strongly in favour of or violently opposed to? Are politicians really strangers to the truth? Would you like to see more honesty in politics?

LANGUAGE FOCUS

Business Grammar

Using the statistics below, complete these sentences describing a country's economic situation:

	1980	1990	Now	3yrs from Now
GDP	$61bn	$130bn	$98	$80
Inflation	21%	16%	18%	23%
Unemployment	6%	12%	15%	20%
Population	34m	32m	36m	39m

1. Since 1980 GDP . . . .
2. Between 1980 and 1990 GDP more than . . . .
3. But for the last . . . . . . years GDP . . . .
4. Over the next 3 years GDP . . . .
5. There's been a 2% rise . . . .
6. Inflation is expected . . . .
7. Compared with 1980, the 1990 inflation figure . . . .
8. Unemployment has been . . . .
9. The most dramatic rise in unemployment . . . .
10. Over the next 3 years unemployment . . . .
11. Compared with . . . . . . years ago, the unemployment situation . . . .
12. In terms of population, the overall trend . . . .
13. In spite of a fall of 2m . . . .
14. The rise in population is expected . . . .
15. Overall, the country is in a worse economic situation than . . . .
16. The outlook for the next . . . .

Word Partnerships 4

Cross out the words which don't fit in the following quotes from a political speech.

1. honestly
    I thoroughly   believe that I was right.
    genuinely

2. totally
    I utterly   refuse to accept that.
    sincerely

3. deeply
    I completely   regret having to do that.
    profoundly

4. distinctly
    I clearly   remember the occasion.
    firmly

5. categorically
    I freely   admit I was to blame.
    openly

If you have done that correctly, you should have crossed out five words which will fit into the quotes below:

6. I . . . . agree with what they say.
7. I . . . . deny having said that.
8. I . . . . hope that we can reach some sort of agreement.
9. I . . . . approve of what they're trying to do.
10. I . . . . maintain that we did the best we could.

Discuss

Think of a strong belief, hope, memory or regret of your own which you don't mind sharing with your colleagues.

FLUENCY WORK

Election Campaign

Country Profile

Study the map below, which depicts the fictitious state of Deltaland and its neighbouring countries. Using the economic statistics from the previous exercise and the information shown here, draw up a profile of the country. What do you think are its economic and political prospects?

Things you might consider include:

- the country's principal industries
- its transport system and infrastructure
- the location of industrial and commercial centres
- natural resources
- environmental hazards
- demographics
- the threat of war from a hostile foreign power
- political unrest at home
- the Northwest-Southeast divide

Outlining Proposals

We are committed to ...
Above all, we must ...
Unless we ...
Provided that we ...
Basically, what we're proposing is ...
In no circumstances must we allow ...
If elected, we aim to ... by ...
We need to be thinking in terms of ...
We see no alternative but to ...
A vote for us will mean ...

Political Strategies

In two weeks time the troubled country of Deltaland is to hold a general election. What political parties do you imagine would exist in such a country? A right wing or nationalist party? A left wing socialist or communist party? A liberal democratic party? A green party?

Work in groups, each representing a different political party. First, hold a strategy meeting to decide on your general policies. Then, in note form, put together a manifesto. Finally, give a five-minute election broadcast to the nation outlining what measures you intend to take to rebuild your country, if elected.

The General Election

Hold the election. You should vote for the party whose policies (apart from those of your own party) you most strongly support. Announce the winning party and interview them on their election victory.

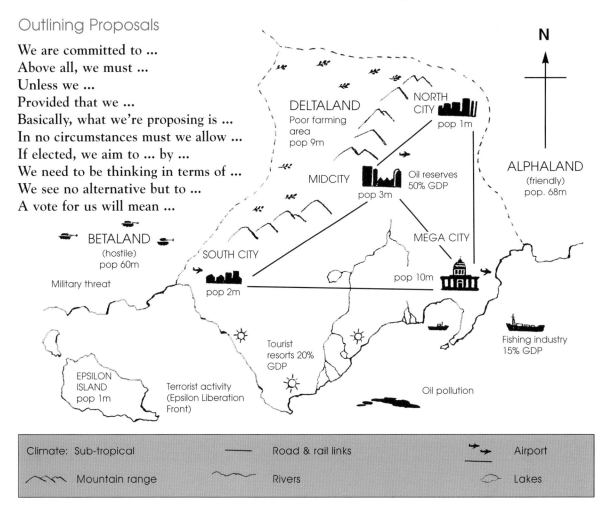

Climate: Sub-tropical   Road & rail links   Airport

Mountain range   Rivers   Lakes

ANSWER KEY

Unit One
Page 11 Crosschecking
2, 3, 6, 7, 8
Page11 Find the Expressions
1. a handful 2. to great effect 3. costs the earth 4. it doesn't always pay to think big
Page 12 Word Partnerships 1
3. create 4. run 5. screen 6. show
Page 12 Word Partnerships 2
marketing drive, advertising slogan, market forces
Page 12 Word Partnerships 3
1. mix 2. leaders 3. expenditure 4. drive 5. campaign 6. segmentation 7. trends 8. shown 9. costs 10. agencies 11. produce 12. run 13. slogans
Page 13 Word Partnerships 4
1. g 2. b 3. h 4. a 5. e 6. j 7. f 8. d 9. c 10. i
Page 13 Quotes
1. market, gap 2. which half 3. advertisement 4. commercials 5. good
Page 14 Word Partnerships 5
1. quite 2. comprehensively 3. exceptionally 4. highly
Page 14 Funny Business
business 1. costly 2. tricky 3. risky 4. shady 5. lengthy
Page 14 Word Grammar
2. internationalize 3. nationalize 4. privatize 5. sensationalize 6. standardize 7. popularize 8. intellectualize 9. categorize 10. computerize 11. legalize 12. generalize 13. commercialize 14. modernize 15. televise
Page 16 Fluency Work, Discuss
1. instant coffee 2. shampoo 3. box of chocolates 4. washing powder 5. soap 6. bar of chocolate 7. cigars 8. aftershave 9. toothbrush 10. tin of chocolates 11. aftershave 12. alcoholic fruit cocktail 13. popcorn 14. babies' nappies 15. paper tissues 16. breakfast cereal 17. white wine 18. condoms 19. perfume 20. strong lager beer 21. anti-spot skin treatment 22. household cleaner 23. processed cheese slices 24. anti-perspirant 25. American rice 26. toothpastes & brushes 27. tinned & packeted Chinese food 28. shampoo 29. sparkling alcoholic drink 30. men's razor

Unit Two
Page 19 Information Check
1, 3, 4
Page 19 Find the Expressions
1. is in 2. in retrospect 3. crackpot 4. made it 5. losing money hand over fist 6. brought ... back from the dead 7. took on 8. a 20th century icon 9. rise through the ranks 10. the budding entrepreneur 11. a flair 12. corporate raider
Page 20 Word Grammar
1. intuitive 2. determined 3. ingenious 4. dynamic 5. dedicated 6. a 7. h 8. f 9. j 10. i
Page 20 Word Partnerships 1
1, 11, 2, 9, 15, 12, 8, 10, 5, 14, 4, 7, 3, 13, 6, 16
Page 21 Word Partnerships 2
1. make 2. starter 3. reliant 4. thrive 5. adapting 6. plan 7. building 8. dealing 9. handle 10. cope 11. stamina 12. minded 13. taking 14. open, suggestions 15. sacrifices, goals

51-75 You are no doubt already aware of your entrepreneurial flair. If you don't already, you could almost certainly work for yourself.

26-50 You have some, but not all, of the skills needed to become an entrepreneur. You should consider your position carefully before launching into a business of your own.

0-25 No doubt, you are an excellent team-member and you would do well to stay where you are. The risks and demands of individual enterprise are not for you.
Page 21 Quotes
1. wanting, get 2. busy 3. per cent, per cent 4. unless 5. first, wife
Page 22 Business Grammar 1
1. b 2. e 3. a 4. f 5. d 6. c; 1. c 2. e 3. f 4. b 5. d 6. a
Page 22 Business Grammar 2
1. The Managing Director stressed the importance of forming a strategic alliance with the Japanese. 2. The Finance Director demanded to know how the project was going to be financed. 3. The Managing Director questioned the need for extra capital. 4. The Finance Director conceded that it was going to take an injection of cash at the outset. 5. The Managing Director reaffirmed his position on the importance of teaming up with the Japanese. 6. The Managing Director recapped on the main points.
Page 23 Business Grammar 3
1. to take 2. losing 3. to get 4. involving 5. concentrating 6. running 7. sacrificing 8. to be 9. to agree 10. to work 11. taking 12. to get 13. drawing 14. to pay 15. having 16. meet 17. to have 18. sending 19. to do 20. meeting
Page 23 Business Grammar 4
1. of leaving 2. for agreeing 3. in meeting 4. in taking 5. on doing 6. for starting 7. from going 8. about taking 9. on being

Unit Three
Page 25 A Girl's Best Friend?
1. d 2. d 3. d 4. d
Page 27 Find the Expressions
1. to loosen its stranglehold 2. their share price takes a tumble 3. throughout its long and chequered history
Page 28 The State of the Market
1. to enter / penetrate / break into the market 2. to be pushed / squeezed out of the market 3. the market has grown 4. the market has shrunk 5. the market is buoyant 6. the market is depressed / has suffered 7. to saturate / flood the market 8. the bottom's dropped out of the market / the market's collapsed 9. the market has dried up
Page 28 Market Expressions
1. buoyant 2. break into / penetrate 3. dominated 4. grew 5. flooded 6. enter 7. saturated 8. collapse 9. depressed 10. suffering 11. entered / penetrated 12. push / squeeze
Page 29 Opposites
1. d 2. e 3. a 4. c 5. f 6. b 7. hardship 8. slump 9. disaster 10. Stockpiling 11. dumping 12. surplus 13. prosperity
Page 29 Word Grammar 1
undercut is the exception; if you undercut someone or undercut someone's prices, you deliberately charge less

ANSWER KEY

than your competitors for similar products or services
a. over/underestimate, over/undervalue, undercut, over/undercharge, over/underprice
b. over/underestimate, over/underrate, over/undervalue, over/understate

Page 30 Word Grammar 2
1. outnumber 2. outselling 3. outbid 4. outclassed
5. outstripped 6. outranks 7. outmanoeuvred
8. outperforms

out means to do better than other products or competitors.

Page 30 Word Partnerships
1. world diamond supply 2. world's greatest cartel
3. chronic cashflow problems 4. massive accumulation of stocks 5. keep prices artificially high 6. saturate the market overnight 7. cut surplus production 8. contain a huge surplus 9. force prices down 10. dump surplus gems onto the market 11. seize control of a company 12. soak up excess supply

Page 32 Follow-up Letter
(model letter) I was most disappointed to read the report in your 'Focus' column on Dec 7 concerning our business practices. When I agreed to speak to your reporters, I never expected to be misrepresented in this way. // There are several inaccuracies in your article which I would like to draw your attention to, and I enclose with this letter a list of factual errors. // Since this article presents our company in such an unfavourable light and since the matter is of considerable public concern, I hope you will seriously consider printing a full retraction. Failing that, I insist that you publish this letter in your next edition. // I look forward to hearing your reaction.

Unit Four

Page 35 Recall
Refer to the article.

Page 35 Find the Expressions
1. trend 2. from scratch 3. really caught on
4. an out-of-work executive 5. management guru
6. restructuring companies from the bottom up
7. may increasingly find itself by-passed altogether
8. has not been able to keep pace with 9. to cut back

Page 36 Word Partnerships 1
1, 7, 9, 2, 5, 11, 3, 6, 10, 4, 8, 12

Page 36 Word Partnerships 2
1. expand 2. restructure 3. downsize 4. streamline
5. merge 6. de-merge 7. diversify 8. take over;
nouns: merger, expansion, takeover, restructuring, diversification, downsizing

Page 37 Word Partnerships 3
1. live up to 2. cut back on 3. get on to 4. keep up with 5. back out of 6. put in for 7. get down to
8. come up with 9. come in for 10. put up with

Page 37 Word Partnerships 4
1. d 2. j 3. h 4. i 5. g 6. b 7. a 8. f 9. c 10. e; extra partnerships: come up with an idea, cut back on overtime, get on to the suppliers, keep up with the competition, back out of a deal, put in for a salary increase, get down to basics, come up to the required standards, come in for most of the blame, put up with appalling conditions

Page 38 Business Grammar 1
1. Well, if we increase wages, the workers will be satisfied. 2. Well, if we freeze wages the workers will be dissatisfied. 3. Well, providing the workers are satisfied, productivity should go up. 4. Well, if the workers are dissatisfied, they might go on strike.
5. Well, providing productivity goes up, turnover will rise too. 6. Well, if the workers take industrial action, turnover will almost certainly fall. 7. Well, if turnover doesn't rise, we'll have to lay off workers.

Page 38 Quotes
1. truth 2. wrong 3. going 4. couldn't 5. blame

Page 39 Business Grammar 2
1. wouldn't + were 2. don't + be 3. be + don't 4. would + could 5. might + let 6. got + suggest 7. didn't + think 8. could + got 9. prefer + mind 10. see + tell

Page 39 Forecasting
1. Promotion prospects are fairly limited. 2. We envisage rapid growth next year. 3. Profits are tipped to reach £600 million. 4. Exxon looks set to take over the company. 5. There's every chance of a management buyout. 6. There's little chance of a merger in the short term. 7. It looks as though the company might break even. 8. The indications are that there'll be mass redundancies. 9. Employment prospects are looking good in the long term. 10. It looks like being a good year for medium-sized companies.

Unit Five

Page 43 Recall
Refer to the article.

Page 43 Response
brand loyalty = what makes the customer continue to buy a well-known brand; brand awareness = how well the customer knows the name of a brand; brandstretching = putting a well-known brand on secondary products to promote the name; own label products = products sold under the retail outlet's own name; me-tooism = the copying by competitor companies of a successful product; subliminal advertising = an indirect method of advertising to the customer on a sub-conscious level; lookalike products = cheap imitations of well-known products; market saturation = when the number of products competing in a market exceeds demand

Page 43 Find the Expressions
1. has now reached fever pitch 2. to slash 3. cut-throat 4. knocked 40c off 5. went to the wall
6. corporate heavyweights 7. turnover 8. mark-up
9. spend a fortune 10. the book value 11. additional revenue 12. a crackdown

Page 44 Word Partnerships 1
1. c 2. a 3. d 4. b 5. h 6. g 7. e 8. f 9. k 10. i 11. l 12. j

Page 44 Word Partnerships 2
market leaders, domination, value, share, saturation

Page 44 Word Partnerships 3
brand war, loyalty, awareness

Page 44 Word Partnerships 4
consumer 1. consumer advertising 2. consumer non-durables 3. consumer goods 4. consumer durables
5. consumer protection 6. consumer research
7. consumer profile

Page 45 Word Partnerships 5
1. brands 2. advertising 3. pouring 4. market, their prices 5. brand 6. consumers, label 17. label, account
8. fight 9. City 10. value 11. names 12. names
13. revenue 14. raised 15. advertising 16. products
17. crackdown 18. saturation 19. consumerism
20. Product 21. fail

ANSWER KEY

Page 46 Business Idioms

a fierce price war, to be under attack from all sides, a hostile environment, a cut-throat struggle just to survive, brand loyalty, campaign, to lose a lot of ground to..., to be completely out-manoeuvred by..., to join forces with..., it's a bit of a long shot, to be an easy target for..., corporate raiders, a takeover battle, to back down, we're not giving in without a fight, to fight off the threat of..., to cut our losses, to withdraw from a market, to reinforce our position, a defensive strategy, to take the offensive, to fight back, to beat the competition, to take on the competition, to win back market share, to take action, to re-group, to change tactics, to mobilize a sales force, an alliance with..., a casualty of the recession

Page 46 Find the Expressions

1. Brand loyalty 2. join forces 3. cut your losses
4. change tactics 5. under 6. struggle 17. ground
8. give in 9. back 10. casualty

Page 47 Business Grammar

1. ever 2. to 3. may / might 4. will 5. not 6. yourself
7. of 8. a 9. obviously / clearly 10. of 11. which
12. a 13. the 14. should 15. more 16. to 17. other
18. as 19. Write / Send 20. According 21. are
22. looking 23. with 24. to 25. make 26. can 27. want
/ need 28. got 29. instead 30. makes 31. all 32. like
33. all 34. you 35. could / might 36. be
37. look 38. such 39. if / since / as / because 40. way

Unit Six

Page 51 Recall
Refer to the article.

Page 51 Find the Expressions
1. strictly speaking 2. pay over the odds 3. money talks

Page 52 Word Partnerships 1
1. goods 2. margins 3. pricing 4. volume 5. profits
6. position 7. profile 8. forces 9. Europe
10. currency 11. trade 12. barriers 13. goods
14. market 15. market

Page 52 Cheap or Expensive?
cheap: 3, 4, 6, 8; expensive: 1, 2, 5, 7, 9

Page 52 Word Grammar
1. Tradeable 2. trading 3. profitable 4. profitability
5. profited 6. competitive 7. competitors
8. competition 9. pricing, price 10. pricey

Page 53 Word Partnerships 2
1. cut 2. fix 3. slash 4. reduce 5. raise 6. quote
7. freeze 8. equalize 9. fixed 10. competitive
11. reasonable 12. attractive 13. elastic 14. unbeatable
15. cut 16. war 17. rise 18. reduction 19. sensitivity
20. elasticity 21. index 22. hike

Page 53 Word Partnerships 3
1. freeze 2. war 3. competitive, unbeatable 4. slashed
5. elastic 6. rise 7. quoted 8. sensitivity

Page 53 Discuss
Margin and *mark-up* are frequently confused. A *mark-up* of 1/3 on goods costing £75 means a retail price of £100. The *gross margin* on this is 25%.

Page 53 Money Expressions
1. Let's talk figures. 2. Just take a look at the figures.
3. Can you give us a rough figure? 4. How did you arrive at these figures? 5. Where did these figures come from? 6. The figures speak for themselves.
7. The figures are not very encouraging. 8. Can you put a figure on it? a. 3 b. 6

Page 54 Word Partnerships 4

Tradeable goods are exported all over the world. Non-tradeables are consumed where they are produced. Too many customers are prepared to pay over the odds. People pay the price they deserve. Product pricing lies at the heart of the marketing process. Its impact is felt in sales volume and profits. Every product occupies a strategic position in the marketplace. A high price often raises a product's profile. A high product profile usually commands a higher price. Economic and market forces are also at work. Prices remain elastic. Most commodities are heavily subsidized. Trade barriers compound the problem. Different rates of tax are imposed on homogeneous commodities. Governments distort prices even further.

(Model summary) Whereas tradeable goods are exported all over the world, non-tradeables are consumed where they are produced. But in both cases too many customers are prepared to pay over the odds and, the fact is, people pay the price they deserve. Because product pricing lies at the heart of the marketing process, its impact is felt in sales volume and profits, and every product occupies a strategic position in the marketplace. A high price often raises a product's profile and a high product profile usually commands a higher price. But economic and market forces are also at work, so prices remain elastic. For one thing most commodities are heavily subsidized, and trade barriers compound the problem. By imposing different rates of tax on homogeneous commodities, governments distort prices even further.

Page 55 Trends 1
1. c 2. f 3. l 4. i. 5. a 6. d 7. b 8. e 9. j 10. g 11. k 12. h

Page 55 Trends 2
group 1: soar, escalate, take off, rocket; group 2: rise, climb; group 3: hold steady, stabilize, flatten out; group 4: drop, fall, decline, slide, dip; group 5: slump, plunge, plummet, crash; group 6: recover, bounce back, pick up, rally; group 7: fluctuate

Unit Seven

Page 57 What's Your Price?
a. = totally incorruptible – are you for real?
b. = you have your principles but are not a slave to them.
c. you see no reason not to take advantage of your good fortune.
d. = utterly unscrupulous – you can certainly be bought, but few people can afford you!

Page 59 Find the Expressions
1. There's no doubt about it. 2. This is a million miles away from... 3. is open to question.

Page 59 Expand
Refer to the article.

Page 60 Summary
1. entertainment 2. luxury 3. contribution
4. marketing 5. scandals 6. extravagant
7. hospitality 8. clients 9. part 10. culture;
a. major b. overall c. staggering d. crucial

Page 60 Word Partnerships
1, 11, 9, 5, 8, 4, 6, 10, 7, 3, 2, 12

Page 61 Describing Food
1. meal 2. food 3. dish 4. meat 5. steak 6. vegetables
7. salad 8. red wine 9. white wine 10. beer

Page 61 Expressions with 'deal'
we reached a deal: 1, 2, 4, 5; we failed to reach a deal: 3, 6, 7, 8

Page 62 The Business Lunch

1. There's a nice new Italian restaurant just round the corner. 2. There's a pretty good Thai restaurant where we usually go. 3. There's a very popular little restaurant which has just opened. 4. There's quite a nice fish restaurant which you might like. 5. There's an excellent vegetarian restaurant which does a wonderful lasagne.

Page 62 Spoken English

1. g 2. a 3. j 4. d 5. h 6. k 7. c 8. e 9. b 10. i 11. f

Unit Eight

Page 65 How Creative Are You?

More than 5 lines = Are you sure you wouldn't be happier in a less intellectually demanding job, like public relations? 5 lines = No prizes for creativity, I'm afraid. The average six year-old could have come up with this solution. 4 lines = You show promise. You've obviously questioned at least one wrong assumption about the task. 3 lines = Well done! You've successfully bent the rules without breaking them, and that's what rules are for. Fewer than 3 lines = Congratulations! You must be cheating. Cheating is highly creative.

Page 67 Find the Expressions

1. is tearing his hair out 2. has backfired
3. a blueprint 4. lucky breaks 5. flopped
6. speaks for itself 7. a climate for creativity
8. it's no coincidence 9. management guru
10. brainstorming session 11. commercial proposition
12. concealing your source

Page 68 Word Partnerships 1

1. f 2. c 3. h 4. j 5. e 6. g 7. b 8. d 9. i 10. a

Page 68 When Do You Say . . .

1. When you say *We've really done our homework on this one*, you mean *We have found out everything we need to know to prepare for this*.
2. When you say *Let's not make a mountain out of a molehill*, you mean *Let's not make this seem more important /serious than it is*.
3. When you say *We'll just have to make the best of a bad job*, you mean *It's a bad situation and we can't change it, so we must do what we can*.
4. When you say *We'll just have to make do*, you mean *Because we haven't got what we really want/need, we must manage as well as we can with what we've got*.

Page 68 Word Partnerships 2

research: fund, carry out, put money into, promote, cut back on; problems: solve, create, face, develop, tackle, define, have, come up against, cause; ideas: implement, generate, develop, brainstorm, promote, come up with, have

Page 69 Word Partnerships 3

1. put money into 2. come up with 3. cut back on
4. generate 5. developed 6. tackle 7. solve
8. implement

Page 69 Word Partnerships 4

MAKE: a decision, money, progress, a breakthrough, a mistake, an impact, a discovery, a comment, an offer, an effort, a profit, a loss, a phone-call, a proposal, arrangements, recommendations, an excuse, an improvement, an appointment, a comparison; DO: business, research, a project, tests, a good job, a rush-job, a feasibility study; MAKE/DO: a survey, a deal, a report, a presentation

Page 70 Word Partnerships 5

1. encouragingly 2. dramatically 3. promisingly
4. slowly

Page 70 Problem Solving

1. e 2. a 3. c 4. g 5. d 6. f 7. b

Page 70 Idea Killers

1. It would cost too much. 2. It would take too long.
3. Our customers would never go for that.
4. We tried that before and it didn't work. 5. I could never get the boss to agree to it. 6. Now isn't the time to be trying anything new. 7. Don't you think we've thought of that already? 8. It's a nice idea but we could never get it to work.

Page 71 The Function of an Executive

1. do 2. done 3. someone 4. way 5. not 6. excuses
7. up 8. incorrectly 9. out 10. left 11. rid 12. children
13. worse 14. oneself 15. place 16. out

Unit Nine

Page 76 Recall

Refer to the article.

Page 76 Word Partnerships 1

1. booming 2. brisk 3. sluggish 4. static 5. plunging

Page 76 Closing the Sale

1. d 2. f 3. e 4. b 5. c 6. g 7. a

Page 76 Word Partnerships 2

1. figures 2. representative 3. technique 4. volume
5. area 6. tax 7. sales representative, sales area 8. sales, static, sales volume 9. sales, sluggish

Page 77 Word Partnerships 3

decision 1. reach, final decision 2. clear-cut decision
3. decision, taken, unanimous 4. makes, snap decisions
5. major decisions, crucial 6. decision, reconsider 7. last-minute decision, right decision 8. decision, reverse

Page 77 Word Partnerships 4

demand 1. boost, stimulate demand 2. meet, satisfy demand 3. gauge demand 4. manage, demand

Page 78 Quotes

customer

Page 78 Presentations 1

1. It's a fact of life. 2. Can you believe it? 3. It's as simple as that. 4. Let me ask you something. 5. I know what you're thinking. 6. But that's just where you're wrong.   7. And that's as true now as it's ever been.
8. And don't let anybody tell you otherwise. 9. I can see some of you know what I'm talking about.
a. 1, 3, 7, 8 b. 2, 4, 5, 9

Page 79 Presentations 2

The Hard Sell 1. d 2. i 3. a 4. f 5. b 6. h 7. c 8. e
9. g The Soft Sell 1. h 2. f 3. d 4. a 5. i 6. b 7. e 8. g 9. c
a. These days, nobody talks about... b. Has it ever struck you...? c. So what it comes down to in the end is... d. Contrary to popular opinion,... e. Did it ever cross your mind...?

Unit Ten

Page 83 Crosschecking

1, 3, 5

Page 83 Find the Expressions

1. to keep your competitive edge 2. to come up with the goods 3. to meet disagreement head on

Page 84 Word Partnerships 1

1. a meeting 2. a minor point 3. good business relationships 4. superiors 5. a deal 6. a decision
7. team-spirit 8. their business 9. their arguments
10. an opinion 11. tension 12. results 13. new ideas
14. information 15. information

Page 84 Word Partnerships 2
1. profit 2. quality 3. price 4. market 5. client
6. technology 7. cost
Page 85 Business Grammar 1
1. g 2. l 3. a 4. j 5. c 6. k 7. e 8. d 9. b 10. h 11. f 12. i
Page 85 Business Grammar 2
1. *Unfortunately* and *I'm afraid* warn the other person that bad news is coming. 2. *Not very / completely / entirely* + a positive adjective sounds friendlier than lots of negative adjectives. Examples: *not very good, not very profitable, not very popular, not entirely true* 3. *That would be a problem* in fact means the same as *That's a problem*, but it sounds less direct. Using *would* suggests that the problem might be solved: *That would be a problem.... unless we can find a solution.* 4. *Quite, rather, slightly* and *somewhat* are softeners. They make bad news sound better. 5. *You said there would be a discount* makes it sound as if you lied! *We understood there would be a discount* means it may just be a misunderstanding. 6. *You don't seem to understand* is strong language but less offensive than *You don't understand.* It allows the possibility that you might understand.
Page 86 Business Grammar 3
1. We understood the goods were on their way.
2. I'm sorry, but we're not very happy about it.
3. That might not be a very good idea. 4. I'm afraid this might not be very convenient. 5. Unfortunately, we're unable to accept your offer.
6. We were hoping for a slightly bigger discount.
7. Your products seem rather expensive. 8. Actually, we were rather hoping to reach agreement today.
9. Unfortunately, it would not be very marketable.
10. I'm afraid there might be a slight delay.
11. Actually, we'd appreciate a little more time.
12. With respect, you don't seem to understand quite how important this is. 13. I'm sure I don't need to remind you of the terms of the contract.
14. I'm afraid we don't seem to be getting very far.

Unit Eleven
Page 91 Crosschecking
1, 5, 6
Page 91 Find the Expressions
1. set them on the road 2. was a by-word for low-quality goods 3. may soon become a thing of the past
Page 91 What Does it Mean?
1. an expert on management 2. a popular and fashionable term 3. an unusual idea, whose main purpose is to attract attention
Page 92 Word Partnerships 1
Refer to the article.
Page 92 Word Grammar
1. production 2. productivity 3. unproductive
4. industrial 5. industrialized 6. industrialists
7. manufacturing 8. manufacturer
Page 93 Word Partnerships 2
1. sell 2. develop 3. manufacture 4. distribute
5. withdraw 6. launch 7. re-launch 8. design
9. modify; chronological order: design, develop, manufacture, launch, distribute, sell, withdraw, modify, re-launch
Page 93 Presenting
(model presentation) The product was originally designed in collaboration with the Japanese and subsequently developed over an 18-month period at our research centre in Birmingham. The product was manufactured at our plant in Bristol and officially launched at the Zurich trade fair. It was then distributed throughout Europe and sold through the main retail outlets. Unfortunately, it had to be withdrawn last month because of complaints about safety. However, certain features have been modified and the product will hopefully be re-launched within six months.
Page 93 Word Partnerships 3
1. hold 2. phase 3. features 4. mass 5. halt
6. methods 7. line 8. speed, step 9. discontinued, went
Page 94 Word Partnerships 4
1. introduction 2. growth 3. maturity 4. saturation
5. decline; 1. introduction 2. stock 3. growth
4. increase 5. maturity 6. stabilize 7. launched
8. saturation 9. exceed 10. decline 11. phased
12. withdrawn
Page 94 Opposites
1. slow down 2. phase in 3. scale down 4. go into production
Page 95 Expressions with 'point'
1. There's no point. 2. Just get to the point!
3. What's the point? 4. OK, you've made your point.
5. That's not the point. 6. You may have a point there.
7. That's just the point. 8. I agree with you up to a point. 9. I don't see the point. 10. There's no point going on about it. 11. That's beside the point.
12. I never did see the point of that.
Page 95 What Do They Mean?
a. 1, 3, 9 b. 5, 11 c. 2 d. 6 e. 8 f. 12 g. 4 h. 10
Page 95 Word Partnerships 5
1. subtle (not obvious), minor (not important)
2. crucial, (extremely important) key (most important), main (most important of several points)
3. question (express doubt or disagreement), query (ask for clarification) 4. raise 5. emphasize

Unit Twelve
Page 99 Crosschecking
1, 3, 5, 6
Page 99 Find the Expressions
1. It's hardly surprising 2. It's a different story 3. It's an overgeneralization
Page 100 Word Partnerships 1
1. f 2. d 3. h 4. a 5. c 6. i 7. b 8. e 9. g
Page 100 Word Partnerships 2
1. run 2. launch 3. set up 4. form 5. join 6. leave
7. sell off 8. wind up 9. float 10. holding 11. parent
12. subsidiary 13. launch, set up, form 14. sell off, wind up 15. a holding or parent company owns more than half the shares in each of its subsidiaries
Page 100 Word Partnerships 3
take off, half-time; 1. recruit, take on 2. lay off, dismiss 3. poach, headhunt 4. headhunt
Page 101 Word Grammar 1
UN- unco-operative, uncompetitive, uncommunicative, unsupportive, unassertive, unskilled, unintelligent, uncreative, unreliable, uncommitted, unapproachable;
IN- indecisive, insincere, insensitive, inarticulate, indiscreet, inconsistent; IM- impractical, impatient;
IR- irresponsible, irrational; DIS- disloyal, dishonest;
Patterns: un- is by far the most common negative prefix; in- is the second most common; im- usually precedes a word beginning with a 'p' (impossible, improbable, impolite); ir- usually precedes a word beginning with an 'r' (irregular, irrelevant, but unreliable)

ANSWER KEY

Page 101 Word Grammar 2
1. sincere 2. assertive 3. articulate 4. reliable
5. approachable 6. committed 7. supportive
8. discreet 9. rational 10. consistent

Page 102 Business Grammar
1. with 2. about 3. on 4. for 5. over 6. between
7. about 8. in / with 9. up 10. up 11. about 12. to
13. up 14. for 15. to 16. in 17. on 18. out 19. on
20. in 21. for 22. up 23. to 24. of 25. about 26. of
27. from 28. in 29. about / on 30. round 31. for 32. on

Page 104 Follow-up Letter
(model letter) Thank you for your application for this
post. // Whilst we were impressed with your
qualifications and experience, and with your
performance at interview, we regret to inform you that
on this occasion you have not been successful. // As
you know, there were a large number of applications
for this post and the standard of applicants was
extremely high. So you should not feel that your non-
selection was due to any failings on your part. // I wish
you every success in your future career. We have put
your details on file and shall consider you for any
suitable vacancies that may arise in our company.

Unit Thirteen

Page 107 Information Check
1, 2, 4, 6

Page 107 Find the Expressions
1. By the turn of the century 2. in charge of your
career 3. are in for a shock

Page 108 Word Partnerships 1
1. c 2. a 3. e 4. d 5. b 6. i 7. h 8. j 9. g 10. f
11. industrial giant 12. bluechip company

Page 108 Word Partnerships 2
1. fast 2. worst 3. far 4. best 5. wide 6. long 7. hard
8. clear

Page 109 Word Partnerships 3
1. product 2. labour 3. guarantee 4. company
5. licence 6. company 7. price 8. accounting
9. deposit 10. customer 11. factor 12. trade 13. loan

Page 109 Word Grammar
1. working 2. unworkable 3. motivator 4. demotivate
5. unemployed 6. unemployable; basic word formation
rules: -able makes a lot of verbs into adjectives, un-
makes a lot of adjectives negative (eg. unemployable,
unworkable, unthinkable, unmarketable, untrainable)

Page 109 Humour
1. look 2. half 3. you

Page 110 Business Grammar 1
Group 1: 1, 4, 8 Group 2: 2, 5, 6, 9 Group 3: 3, 11
Group 4: 7, 10, 12

Page 111 Are You a Workaholic?
0-20 points = There's no danger of you becoming a
workaholic. In fact, quite the reverse! 21-40 points =
You seem to have the balance between work and play
about right. 41-60 points = Watch the blood pressure!
60-80 points = Congratulations! You're a workaholic.
Isn't there some work you should be getting on with?

Unit Fourteen

Page 115 Crosschecking
1, 2, 3, 6, 7

Page 115 Find the Expressions
1. doing our bit 2. the track record 3. wreck
livelihoods 4. bribery 5. insider trading
6. antagonistic to

Page 116 Word Partnerships 1
1. consumption 2. resources 3. hemisphere
4. technology 5. employment 6. security
7. inequality 8. war 9. dynamics 10. goods
11. nature 12. quality 13. restoration
14. programme 15. systems 16. earth 17. society
18. acts 19. users 20. circumstances

Page 116 Word Partnerships 2
1. issues 2. waste 3. terms 4. individual 5. business
6. economy 7. system 8. trend 9. disaster 10. plan
11. record 12. technology 13. strength 14. crime
15. trading 16. powers 17. degradation 18. reach

Page 117 Business Grammar 1
1. *We don't have to spend more money on this* is the
answer to both questions (don't have to = it's not
necessary) 2. *We must cut down on waste* is more likely
to be my opinion (here, must = internal obligation).
We have to cut down on waste might be an order from
someone else. 3. *I needn't have finished the report*, the
use of the present perfect indicates that the report has
been completed unnecessarily. 4. *That wouldn't be
enough* is more diplomatic. 5. That must be right.
6. We couldn't have known what would happen.
7. We could do it if we tried (here, could = would be
able to). 8. If he calls, tell him I'm out (here, if he
should call = if he happens to call) 9. *You could ask her
but she won't know yet* is clearly not about future time
(here, won't know = is certain not to know). *You could
ask her but she won't help you* may be a prediction, but
it is probably more of a description of how unhelpful
'she' is: she'll refuse to help you because she always
refuses to help people (here, she won't help you = she's
not 'willing' to help).

Page 117 Word Partnerships 3
1. the environment 2. pollution 3. resources
4. an issue 5. a promise 6. a policy 7. a goal
8. power

Page 118 Business Grammar 2
1. d 2. j 3. a 4. f 5. h 6. c 7. i 8. b 9. g 10. e

Page 118 Business Grammar 3
1. I shouldn't think so. I might have known! I
wouldn't be surprised. I must be mad! 2. I wouldn't
like to say. I couldn't agree more. I can understand
how you feel. I could be wrong, of course. 3. You must
be joking! You can't be serious! You could be right.
You should have known better. 4. You can say that
again! You should have told me sooner. You needn't
have bothered. You may have a point there. 5. We'll
never know. We'll have to wait and see. We can't be
certain. 6. It wouldn't surprise me. It shouldn't be a
problem. It couldn't have come at a worse time. It
might just be the best thing we ever did. 7. There'd be
no point. There must be a way round this. There
wouldn't be time.

Unit Fifteen

Page 123 Information Check
1, 3, 5

Page 123 Find the Expressions
1. to see the colour of your money 2. it's a no-win
situation 3. cut your losses

ANSWER KEY

Page 124 Word Partnerships 1
1, 5, 7, 10, 4, 3, 8, 11, 9, 2, 6, 12

Page 124 Going Bankrupt
2. To go like a bomb means to go very fast or to be very successful

Page 124 Expressions with 'money'
1. waste 2. bad 3. tied 4. tight 5. liquid 6. throw
7. ploughing 8. made

Page 125 Word Partnerships 2
1. to demand immediate payment 2. to regulate business-to-business relations 3. to put pressure on debtors 4. to minimize the risk of bad debt 5. to damage customer relations 6. to insist on money in advance 7. to ease the cashflow situation 8. to process letters of credit 9. to run a credit check 10. to charge interest on oustanding debts 11. to risk alienating customers 12. to finance new projects

Page 125 Word Partnerships 3
1. win 2. lose 3. handle 4. process 5. receive 6. place
7. cancel 8. phone or fax through 9. dispatch 10. new
11. bulk 12. emergency 13. repeat 14. regular
15. place, received, processed, dispatch 16. win, handled, cancelling, lose

Page 126 Business Grammar
1. in 2. by 3. on 4. in 5. on 6. on 7. on 8. up 9. off
10. in 11. behind 12. off 13. up 14. by 15. in

Page 126 Humour
1. e 2. d 3. c 4. a 5. b

Page 128 Follow-up Letter
(model letter) I am again writing to you with regard to the outstanding sum of £[amount] owed by your company to Halliday Electronics. As I have written to you on this matter on two previous occasions, you must be aware that your account is now [number] months in arrears, and so far we have received no payment whatsoever. // Perhaps you could inform us of the reason for this delay. If it is merely the result of an administrative error, we would appreciate the prompt resolution of whatever problems you may be having. // We sincerely hope that your company is not experiencing difficulties of a more serious nature, and, whilst we have always enjoyed an excellent relationship with [name of company], I am afraid that we must now insist on immediate settlement. Otherwise, I shall have no alternative but to refer the matter to our legal department. // I trust you will give this matter your urgent attention.

Unit Sixteen

Page 131 Information Check
1, 3, 6, 8

Page 131 Find the Expressions
1. no one has a clue 2. industrial might 3. are on the verge of economic collapse 4. crippling deficits 5. to be tightened 6. an influx 7. dead-end jobs 8. it goes without saying, 9. the pound is fragile

Page 132 Word Partnerships 1
1. falling 2. clue 3. even 4. unemployment
5. statistics 6. close 7. recession 8. collapse 9. threat
10. labour 11. wage 12. reaching 13. answer
14. declining 15. recovery

Page 132 Word Partnerships 2
1. growth 2. indicators 3. crisis 4. forecast 5. forces
6. theory 7. policy 8. outlook 9. recession 10. measures
11. development 12. ruin 13. reform 14. strategy
15. recovery 16. union 17. sanctions 18. aid

Page 132 Word Partnerships 3
1. indicators, forecasts 2. ruin 3. outlook
4. recession, measures 5. union

Page 133 Current Affairs 1
1. privatize 2. cut 3. come out of 4. improve 5. relax
6. scrap 7. close 8. break off 9. harm 10. impede
11. reduce 12. divide 13. push up 14. help 15. resist
16. put off 17. launch 18. pay off 19. adopt 20. neglect

Page 133 Current Affairs 2
1. recession 2. trade gap 3. social benefits
4. immigration controls 5. scrapped 6. recession
7. our image abroad 8. pressure 9. foreign investors
10. attack 11. unemployment 12. Public opinion

Page 133 Abbreviations
1. annual general meeting 2. International Monetary Fund 3. gross national product 4. gross domestic product 5. North American Free Trade Agreement
6. General Agreement on Trade and Tariffs 7. retail price index 8. value added tax

Page 134 Word Grammar 1
1. e 2. h 3. a 4. f 5. c 6. g 7. d 8. b; pro- / anti - European, nuclear, terrorist, fascist, government; anti-war; pre- / post- industrial, war; post-communist era; non- conformist,essential, specialist; ex- wife, terrorist, government; neo-fascist; multi-lateral, media, national

Page 134 Word Grammar 2
1. economist 2. economical 3. economize 4. politicians
5. politically 6. politicized

Page 135 Business Grammar
(model answers) 1. has increased by over 50%
2. doubled 3. has fallen 4. is expected to fall by a further $12bn 5. in inflation 6. to rise 7. was relatively encouraging 8. steadily increasing 9. was between 1980 and 1990 10. is likely to be pushed up by a further 5% 11. is considerably worse 12. is upward 13. between 1980 and 1990, the population is now growing rapidly 14. to continue over the next three years 15. it was in 1990 16. three years is not encouraging

Page 135 Word Partnerships 4
1. thoroughly 2. sincerely 3. completely 4. firmly
5. categorically 6. completely 7. categorically
8. sincerely 9. thoroughly 10. firmly

TEACHERS' INFORMATION FOR UNIT 6

The Commodities Game: Updates

Update 1

Current Prices:	Gold 400	Silver 5	Copper 2500	Tin 5000	Coffee 3500	Sugar 300	Oil 20

Forecast: In the short term, a rising price index is likely to push up the price of gold as a hedge against inflation, but long-term prospects are much less attractive. Copper looks promising. We're not predicting much movement in tin, coffee, sugar or oil. Risk-takers should take a chance on silver.

Update 2

Current Prices: Gold up at 450   Silver down at 4.50   Copper down at 2000   Tin stable at 5000
Coffee stable at 3500   Sugar down at 275   Oil down at 19

Forecast: Gold is still very much in demand and the price will probably continue to climb. Copper looks disappointing. Tin looks set to remain firm at 5000 but rumours of crop damage may boost the price of coffee and sugar. Oil prices should recover in the short term. Our advice is to go long on silver.

Update 3

Current Prices: Gold up at 525   Silver stable at 4.50   Copper up at 3000   Tin stable at 5000
Coffee up at 4000   Sugar down at 250   Oil up at 20

Forecast: The bubble must burst soon for gold as inflation rates start to come down. Copper is again a good investment. The tin market is still showing no movement at all and long-term prospects are poor. We remain confident that a reduced world supply of coffee and sugar will escalate prices. Brave speculators will hang on to silver which will eventually come good. Buy oil.

Update 4

Current Prices: Gold down at 450   Silver down at 3.25   Copper down at 2500   Tin stable at 5000
Coffee up at 4500   Sugar down at 200   Oil down at 18

Forecast: As predicted, the price of gold has slipped back and the indications are that it will continue to slide. Although we've not had much success forecasting the price of copper, we now firmly expect it to fall. Hold coffee and sugar. Oil should bounce back to somewhere in the region of $21 a barrel. Silver must soon turn the corner as industrial demand begins to exceed supply. Sell tin.

Update 5

Current Prices: Gold down at 225   Silver up at 3.50   Copper up at 3500   Tin down at 2000
Coffee stable at 4500   Sugar down at 150   Oil up at 22

Forecast: If you've been taking our advice you will by now have sold all your gold. Buy it back - it's about to stage a recovery. Also buy tin. Silver has picked up only slightly but get ready for a price explosion here. Copper too will perform well. Coffee may have reached a ceiling at 4500 but our advice is to hold. Sugar is proving to be a poor investment. Sell oil.

Update 6

Current Prices: Gold up at 300   Silver up at 5.50   Copper down at 2000   Tin stable at 2000
Coffee up at 6000   Sugar up at 200   Oil up at 26

Forecast: Go short on gold - there's still room for further improvement. Buy silver - it's about to go through the roof! The bottom really has dropped out of the copper market, so get rid of holdings in copper. The clever money's on tin which looks set to double in price. Coffee surely cannot exceed an all-time high of 6000. Sell sugar. Problems in the Middle East may trigger a rise in the price of oil.

Update 7

Current Prices: Gold up at 350   Silver up at 10   Copper up at 3500   Tin up at 4000
Coffee stable at 6000   Sugar up at 250   Oil up at 38

Forecast: The trend for gold prices is now downward. Sell all holdings in gold. Take a chance on copper. Sell coffee. Sell sugar. Buy oil - even at this high price, the worsening situation in the Middle East should push it higher. Buy tin - it's about to go sky high. The silver market's going crazy! Buy as much silver as you can afford before it takes off.

Update 8

Current Prices: Gold down at 300   Silver up at 25   Copper down at 2500   Tin up at 7000
Coffee stable at 6000   Sugar up at 300   Oil down at 22

Forecast: If you have any gold left, sell it. It's going to fall through the floor. Those who like to live dangerously should take a risk on silver. It's ridiculously high now but it could go even higher. Sell copper. Sell tin. Sell sugar. Sell coffee - it's reached its peak and must now fall. Apologies for our previous misinterpretation of the oil market. A surprise peace deal in the Middle East means that oil prices will continue to drop back and may even hit an all-time low. It's time to sell.

Final Update

Current Prices: Gold down at 200   Silver up at 50   Copper up at 3000   Tin down at 3500
Coffee up at 8500   Sugar up at 400   Oil down at 17

Now calculate your total assets by adding your remaining capital to the current value of your holdings. Have you made a profit or a loss? Who made the most money? Did you notice any clear trends in commodity prices? Did they help you to make your investment decisions?